YOUTUBE PLAYBOOK 2021

THE PRACTICAL GUIDE & SECRETS FOR GROWING YOUR CHANNEL, MAKING MONEY AS A VIDEO INFLUENCER, MASTERING SOCIAL MEDIA MARKETING & THE BEGINNERS WORKBOOK (+ 10 TIPS)

BRANDON'S BUSINESS GUIDES

CONTENTS

Part III
CREATING YOUTUBE VIDEOS

Part IV

MANAGING YOUR YOUTUBE
CHANNEL

Part V
MONETIZE YOUR YOUTUBE CHANNEL

INTRODUCTION

When I published my first book on YouTube marketing, many of my readers were thrilled to finally have a simple, easy to read playbook that would enable them to learn the basics of this giant platform. It has done well in serving that purpose. But as we all know, the Novel Coronavirus hit in 2020 and set the world into a global pandemic that we are yet to recover from.

The impact of the global pandemic has been experienced in every niche, both online and offline. Even YouTube felt the pressures of the changing world. It made many adjustments, including issuing out a report that there would be an increased number of deleted and banned videos during the pandemic season. Why does this matter to you?

The simple reason that whether we like it or not, the world as we knew it in 2020 no longer exists. The game has changed dramatically in just a matter of months. Those entering the world of social media or those who want to win in this new environment of 2021 will have to switch up their game.

I am assuming you picked up this book because you're among the smart people who recognize that change is already in the air. Unfortunately, that makes a lot of the information you might come across on the Internet pretty out-dated. That includes all the awesome books that have been written in the past about how to win big with YouTube marketing (including my first edition). I'm not saying these books have no value, but I insist we need to have fresh approaches and strategies to help us in this new world.

One thing hasn't changed. YouTube remains a powerful platform for anyone of any age, ethnicity, background, vocation, and in any location to share their message and build significant influence. So even if you're just starting out now, there's still plenty of time for you to carve out a successful spot in the minds and hearts of your eagerly awaiting YouTube community.

To fully utilize the power of YouTube this year so you can start a successful channel around your passion and effectively grow your business or reach your goals, you're going to need a solid plan.

There was a time when the only thing a YouTube creator needed to do to enter stardom was simply switching on a camera and ranting about whatever comes to mind. Done consistently and with a bit of entertainment, many channels have grown to massive numbers with obsessive fans and dismissive naysayers helping to keep that fire alive for the ambitious YouTuber. If that's the kind of imagery you hold in your mind about how your path of success will be, I'm sorry, but you're in for a rude awakening.

Sure, there was a time when winging, it was good enough, but that time has passed.

As you begin this journey, realize that it will take commitment, discipline, and a solid plan on your end to reach those lofty goals. If you are looking to learn how to develop these things, then you're definitely in the right place.

I've realized since releasing my first book on YouTube that people beginning this journey don't know where their attention and energy should go or how to grow their channel, let alone create passive income. And since there are so many paths to take, most end up overwhelmed, frustrated, and even give up too soon. Others overcomplicate things, which leads to unnecessary mistakes. Ever heard of the saying 'don't take the slow boat to China'?

Well, I'm here to make sure you don't take the slow boat to China.

The purpose of this book is to help you avoid the many mistakes I've made while growing my YouTube channel and marketing my business. I want to share the processes and hacks that I learned the hard way with you so that you can achieve your goals faster than I ever did.

Years ago, when I started my journey, I could have used a book like this. At the time, there wasn't much clarity on how to develop a solid plan for YouTube success. If you've read my first YouTube book, you know it was anything but rosy when I first set up my channel. At first, I created video content and hosted it on YouTube because I wanted to give my blogging audience some variety in the content I produced. After about eighteen months of randomly posting videos and embedding them on my blog, I decided to take YouTube seriously. Vlogging was becoming a common term. I could see YouTube creators popping up everywhere and claiming to generate massive income from video content creation alone.

When I jumped into the deep end, I assumed things would pick up instantly since I had already been publishing a few videos here and there, and I had a pretty good blog follow-ing. Boy, was I wrong. Three years into my endeavors, and I still couldn't gain much momentum.

Most people would have given up after the first year, not me. The more I researched the channels that were doing well, the more I was convinced that I could make this work too... but how?

It took a while to realize that I was making many rookie mistakes, which cost me the channel's growth and success. Painstaking effort and hard lessons learned, combined with my persistent attitude, and finally enabled me to have my breakthrough. But it took years! I want to shave off some of that learning curve for you and pass on some of the applied and proven knowledge that I have acquired over the years. Today I have a healthy subscriber community of several hundred thousand followers. But I can still recall how hard it was to hit those first one thousand subscribers. If you can persist long enough to reach your first 1,000 followers on YouTube, you'll be on your way to creating any kind of success you desire.

This book is an expansion from my last that will equip you with all the tools you need, whether you read the first book or not. To execute this objective successfully, you need some support. I can promise you that as you trust in the process, I am sharing in this book, and as you take consistent massive action, you will experience growing YouTube success. It won't happen overnight. YouTube is not an overnight game, especially not in 2021 and beyond, but success is still possible.

Many aspiring YouTube superstars, influencers, and entrepreneurs who want to acquire business through this channel start their channel without learning some key ingredients that are a pre-requisite for success. Doing this blindly will only cause you to fall into the same pit of despair that most of us know all too well. If I can save you the time and trouble that usually accompanies a lack of know-how, would that be meaningful to you?

Suppose I can show you exactly where to place your energy and attention and the things you need to learn to become successful on YouTube. Will you commit all the way starting now?

Then let's get started because we have much ground to cover. In this book, you'll learn the ingredients needed to create successful videos, strategies, and hacks that help you attract and earn new views even if no one knows you yet. You'll learn how to make money as an influencer and how to create passive income from all your content creation efforts. Whether you want to be a superstar or a successful business owner driving sales through YouTube marketing, this book has it all, and you get to use it to your advantage. Take notes, implement everything you learn, and remember to trust in this process. YouTube success is a journey, even for those who end up becoming overnight superstars.

I

UNDERSTANDING YOUTUBE

WHAT YOU NEED TO KNOW BEFORE GETTING STARTED

*S*uppose you're going to invest the next few months and years establishing your brand on the YouTube platform. In that case, it makes sense to learn a little about the platform's origins and what makes it so unique. Like for example, did you know YouTube started off as a dating platform? Few people know this, but co-founder Steven Chen said it was initially designed for dating so that people could upload videos of themselves talking about their dream partner.

In this chapter, we will cover a little bit of YouTube's history, present, and future, as well as why it's both a social platform search engine. We will also get a bit technical by introducing you to the robust YouTube algorithm so you can create your channel and content with the understanding necessary to help your videos perform well.

YouTube is a unique social networking platform for this simple reason. It's both a social networking channel and a search engine. So it falls into the category of social media, yet it's also far grander if you think about it. But how did it become this big giant? Surely, it's not just because the Internet giant Google owns it. Right you are! This is why it's best to start with an overview of YouTube's past, present, and future so you can align yourself with this ever-growing social and search engine platform.

YOUTUBE: THE PAST, THE PRESENT, AND THE FUTURE

Few people know this, but YouTube came to be due to a combined effort from three former PayPal employees. Chad Hurley, Steven Chen, and Jawed Karim believed that ordinary people would enjoy sharing personal homemade videos. So they created the first website version of what we know today in early February of 2005. The beta version was launched in May of 2005 and already started attracting 30,000 visitors per day. Yes, that was a massive number at the time. By the time it was officially launched in December of 2005, the platform was getting over two million video views per day. By January 2006, those numbers increased to more than 25 million views. A few months later (March 2006), the platform had more than 25 million uploaded videos with more than 20,000 videos being uploaded daily. Even back then, these were huge numbers. The platform has shown no signs of slowing down since its launch. When it comes to funding, the original founders got their first real funding in November 2005 from Sequoia Capital, which invested more than $3 million. Of course, with the massive growth I just shared, it wasn't too long before popularity took over, and Google decided it was time to take their lion's share. In November of 2006, Google bought YouTube for a cool $1.65 billion. Yes, that was a B (billion), not a million.

Fast forward years of successful growth, more popularity, and lots of stardom case studies from YouTube creators who gained fame and fortune, YouTube has not shown any signs of slowing down. But their early days were rather humble. In the early days, YouTube was very "homely" and raw. You'd find hilarious pranks, videos showing interesting locations, crazy stunts, and neighborhood entertainment. There were only square videos available at that time. But with time, the platform matured and expanded to include political debates, unfiltered war footage, musical performances, instructional videos, lots more comedy, and entertainment. In 2007, YouTube partnered up with CNN to create an opportunity for ordinary citizens to interact with potential United States presidential candidates, which exponentially grew the platform's engagement.

VIDEO PROGRESS ON YOUTUBE

The first video ever published is said to be **on the 23rd of April 2005** by one of the founders titled "**Me At The Zoo**." Since then, YouTube has gone from zero to 1 billion views in under a decade. According to Statista, YouTube currently has 2 billion users worldwide and growing. (Statista, 2019). It, therefore, stands to be the biggest social network - even bigger than Facebook.

It is still considered by many to be the easiest platform to share video content with a broad audience. Setting up a channel and getting started is fast and simple, as you'll learn in an upcoming section. With a good strategy, you can be unknown today and reaching millions of views around the world by the end of the week.

You can easily reach people of any age group today on YouTube because research shows that both the young and older people using the Internet are also watching videos on YouTube. Since most people prefer to consume visual content, the growth of YouTube and your ability to succeed have no limits. But what about in the future? What are some of the predictions being made?

THE FUTURE OF YOUTUBE

Video is still expected to remain front-and-centre in our society. It has become the most effective strategy anyone can use to connect with an audience. You don't even need fancy equipment or a professional studio to do so.

Many smartphone users find engaging types of video content difficult to resist, and I believe this will continue to be the case. Why? Because according to recent data, 85% of Internet users in the U.S watch video content. And in 2021, it is expected that the average person will spend 100 minutes daily watching online videos! That's a 19% increase since 2019.

While it's hard for anyone to accurately prophecy where any of these social networking platforms will be in another decade, there seems to be enough reason to assume YouTube won't be going anywhere, anytime soon. There's a strong chance that today's YouTuber's will become tomorrow's moguls. The Internet and the digital economy are still in infancy. We know the best is yet to come, and those that learn to ride this wave with YouTube might just continue to experience tremendous success regardless of the new adaptations the platform brings about.

Consider people like PewDiePie (Felix Kjellberg). He is arguably the most famous YouTuber on the planet generating billions of views from his channel. With all the fame and money he's acquired over the years, it's unlikely he would sizzle out easily. In fact, according to an interview with The Guardian Magazine a while back, PewDiePie hinted that he's contemplating expanding out into creating a multi-channel network at some point. There's a good chance many of these YouTubers who have become influencers are more likely to seek out television stardom as well or even develop their own networks. Imagine any kind of future you'd like to have, and I can assure you, YouTube can become a vehicle for that accomplishment.

As for the platform itself, given that its parent company is Internet goliath Google - I'm inclined to believe it will continue to evolve, adapt, and invest in further growth within the platform itself.

When the platform launched, it only had square videos and no advertising opportunities. Over the years, it has evolved and expanded to include a very robust advertising system. The video formats have also been evolving. It's wise for every YouTuber to keep up with these ever-changing video requirements. As an overview, YouTube allows you to upload various sizes ranging from 240p to 2160p(4K).

- 240p: 426x240 pixels
- 360p: 640x360 pixels

- 480p: 854x480 pixels
- 720p: 1280x720 pixels
- 1080p: 1920x1080 pixels
- 1440p: 2560x1440 pixels
- 2160p: 3840x2160 pixels

That means if you're just learning his stuff, you can upload a video size that's as little as 426X240 pixels or go as large as 3840X2160 pixels. But, dimension isn't the only thing you need to get right. You also need to consider video size, length, and aspect ratio, especially now that they also added new features such as vertical video stories.

We're going to dive deeper into the different video sizes available, whether you're running ads or posting organically for your channel so stay tuned for those fresh updates and features in an upcoming chapter. For now, realize that it's going to be essential to use the recommended video size and to keep refreshing yourself on the latest changes. Why?

Because if you want to attract more views and make more profit, you need to use the correct YouTube video size. Failure to do so will result in low-quality content, which will repel the audience you're looking to attract. For that reason, I encourage you to regularly visit the content creator academy webpage, where they have all things YouTube related.

YOUTUBE AS A SOCIAL MEDIA PLATFORM

Do you know why YouTube is considered a social media platform? Well, to effectively answer that, let's focus on clarifying what an online social network is. An online social network is a platform where you and other like-minded people can connect. You can build relationships, exchange and share information, etc. YouTube is a platform that enables you to do all that, and so much more. Not only can you build new connections, but you can also learn from new people who are halfway across the world from you. When a social network is done right, it becomes a thriving ecosystem where content creators, brands, and users benefit from being actively engaged on the platform. I'd say YouTube has done a fantastic job creating such an environment.

One of the critical factors to consider when labeling YouTube as a social media platform comes from this simple word - community.

There is a massive community on YouTube of people who are producing, sharing, and consuming content. The most active and engaged people on the platform feel like they are part of something bigger, like they belong. These people support each other, hang out together, and share common values. That, my friend, is called community building. It may not be a community in the traditional offline sense of the word where everyone is physically next to each other, but it is nonetheless.

Because YouTube is a social media platform, it's not enough to occasionally post videos and pray to the traffic gods that your channel will attract people. It's also not a great idea to focus solely on data and getting views on your video. The approach should be the same as any other social networking site. You need to focus on connecting with and interacting with the people you wish to have as part of your YouTube community. We will talk more in-depth about how you can actually do this, but it is essentially about posting quality videos with content that your ideal audience will find valuable. Like other social channels, you can send out friend requests, ask people to subscribe to your channel, and engage in live chats, especially when you do live streaming. More on that later.

The other thing I love about YouTube is the fact that you can create real conversations around your video content. Since most people spend a lot of time watching videos on the platform, if you engage and interact with community members by asking questions on the comments and making sure you reply to all the comments people make, you can demonstrate to your new audience that you care. And they, in turn, will follow and consume what you have to offer. The more value and engagement you bring to this social network, the more success you will experience, especially as a business owner.

YOUTUBE AS A SEARCH ENGINE PLATFORM

A while back, Google (the parent company that owns YouTube) released a resource that answers many of the questions we all ask when we decide to set up a YouTube channel. Namely, how exactly does YouTube work?

While I'm sure they didn't spill all their secrets, they have given us enough knowledge that we can leverage to our advantage. I will be taking more about the YouTube algorithm and hacks to help you rank higher on their search engine in a later chapter. But for you to get the most of that conversation, you need to understand that YouTube is a search engine just like Google, Yahoo, etc. There's a tremendous amount of organic traffic to be enjoyed within YouTube's own platform because many people actually use that search bar. Besides that fact, we also have the added benefit of being favored highly by Google when they rank content on the homepage. Videos from YouTube always rank high on a Google search page, and I don't know if you noticed, but Google added a new tab specifically titled "video." So when it comes to doing the regular search, people are still being served video results for their query. Let me put this practically for you so you can understand the power of this.

Suppose your potential client is looking for a service you can offer. They head over to Google and type in their query. Millions of results show up in the form of regular articles. But they see a tab "video" and click on that because let's face it; most people prefer to watch than read. Videos are not as saturated as text-based solutions. Since you're smart, you have a video explainer showing them exactly how to solve their need and how you do it fast and affordably. What do you think are the chances of getting that cold lead and converting a customer?

I'd say, pretty high. You don't need a big audience or a huge channel. What you need is to understand how to leverage YouTube.

HOW YOUTUBE SEARCH WORKS

The search ranking system on YouTube is pretty amazing because it sorts through over 500 hours of content that gets uploaded every minute. Then it finds the most relevant results for the search query given by the end-user. Thanks to Google's information, we know there are three main elements you need to focus on: quality, relevance, and engagement.

Quality:

That refers to how authoritative your channel and content are for the target audience. YouTube wants expert, authoritative, and trustworthy content for its community members. That's why I always recommend starting narrow with a specific topic. It's a lot easier to prove that your channel is worth being promoted when you focus on delivering quality content on what you know really well.

The more you can deliver that, the better your videos will perform. "...

Relevance:

YouTube's algorithm is still a mystery even for the so-called expert hackers. But what we all know for sure is that being relevant is a critical factor for channel growth. There are many indicators the algorithms look for to determine whether something is relevant to an audience or not, some of which include the video content itself (though not 100% perfect), title, description, and tags.

Engagement:

The last thing I want us to discuss here that the algorithm cares about is video engagement. Watch time is especially critical for the algorithm because it uses that as a key indicator of whether to continue promoting your content or not. The more people watch and stay on the platform thanks to your video, the more they will promote your stuff to a bigger audience.

OTHER FACTORS THAT ARE A MUST-KNOW

In the same earlier mentioned report, YouTube shared that they care a lot about promoting authoritative content from reliable sources. But only when it is appropriate. So when it comes to scientific, political, medical information, or breaking news, they will promote the most credible channels and personalities on the platform.

The key thing to take away from this is that you need to build credibility. You do not have to be Oprah or CNBC, but you do need to demonstrate to the algorithm that your content can be trusted. This is especially true if you are dealing with educational type of content. This may not apply as much with entertainment or music channels because what matters most in such cases is popularity, freshness, and relevancy, which we already discussed.

Recommended videos

This is an exciting one for me because it offers us a window of opportunity to do well right off the bat. Have you ever noticed the "recommended" icon when watching content on YouTube? You can usually see it in the section titled "Up

Next" on your dashboard. This is YouTube's way of suggesting what you should consume next. The algorithm factors in many things before making that recommendation, including: what channels you're subscribed to, your watch history, the time of day, and so on. Getting your video to appear on this recommended list will be a huge win, and it will accelerate your channel growth. I even have hacks that will increase your chances of showing up on that suggestions list.

Before we can move on, I'd also like to emphasize that YouTube does factor in personalization when determining what to show a user. If you've noticed how many times recommended videos show up based on your recent activity, this will make sense. As a user, your homepage gets populated by more of the things you've watched, liked, and interacted with. Flip perspective for a bit and think like a creator. The more you can create content that a user interacts with, the more of your stuff he or she will be served by YouTube. Therefore, it is imperative to create content with your ideal consumer in mind. You want to create content you feel confident he or she will want to click on, watch, and like. That's your golden ticket to the success you desire on this platform.

Want to get more technical about how the YouTube algorithm works?

If what I just shared wasn't sophisticated enough for you, I've got something that will satisfy the tech geek in you. There's a research paper published by Google engineers Paul Covington, Jay Adams, and Emre Sargin. They break down the signals they use to rank videos for YouTube recommendations. If you can recall, recommendations are a pretty huge deal when it comes to getting more people to know about your channel. In the paper, they talk about the following:

1. Click-through rate. That refers to the likelihood of someone clicking on your video after they've seen it.
2. Watch time. That refers to the total amount of time that viewers spend watching your videos.
3. How many videos the user has watched from your channel.
4. How recently the user watched a video about the same topic.
5. What the user has searched for in the past.
6. The user's previously watched videos.
7. The user's demographic information and location.

Want to read the entire research paper (Deep Neural Networks for YouTube Recommendations)? Check out the resource section for links.

ACTIVITY #1: EXPLORING YOUTUBE

Now it's time to start taking some action. Before getting into the next chapter, it's good to familiarize yourself with this platform through the lens of the new insights and lessons learned. So here's what you're going to do.

Open an incognito webpage, sign in to your personal YouTube if you have one, and start browsing. First, begin by entering the homepage and playing around with the search bar at the top. Type in a query around your topic of expertise or whatever your channel will be about. Observe how many search results come up. Notice which top channels are being promoted and look at their titles, length of the video, number of views, year of publication, and quality of the content. I also want you to check the sidebar menu and notice what YouTube recommends to you. Browse the platform from the eyes of a consumer, your potential subscriber.

Before moving on, the last activity is to type in the same search query on the main Google search tab then hover over to "videos." Notice how many of the videos you encountered on YouTube are showing up here. What you learn from exploring YouTube through this new lens will equip you as we move forward.

2

WHY YOUTUBE?

*B*y now, it should be evident that YouTube is on fire. Billions of users log in every month to consume content. There are also as many content creators or YouTubers in the backend, pushing out hundreds of content every minute of the day. The amount of activity taking place on this platform can feel quite overwhelming. The fact that you can find almost any topic on any genre can make one wonder why they should even consider setting up a channel. Everything is already there, right?

Yes and no. There's indeed a lot of content on almost any topic you might have in mind. Still, the reality is, you are a unique individual. Even if you start a channel with a common topic, as long as you remain true to yourself, it won't be like any other channel because no one can imitate you. That is what makes YouTube special. There's enough room for every content creator. The only obstacle you have is figuring out how to be more of yourself, so your content stands out.

The question you need to be asking isn't why should I invest my time, resources, and energy on YouTube when over 500 hours of video are uploaded every minute. Instead, it should be a question directed to your own self-expression as a unique human being. Meaning - what am I extremely passionate about that I also feel I can become an authoritative voice for?

Most people who start a channel do so out of sheer passion and an urge to share their message with the world, but that's not the only reason to become a YouTuber. You could also do it because you want to become famous like the Kardashians or to generate income. I don't think there's a wrong or right reason, but I believe there should be a big enough reason.

Always start by identifying your "why" for taking this decision to create a successful channel because you will need the fuel when the going gets tough. So here are some of the reasons I know of for starting a successful YouTube channel.

- To express your passion and share your message with the world.
- For money.

- For fame.

FOR PASSION

If you want to use this platform to express yourself and share your passions with the world, you're not alone. Many of the channels that have successfully grown to millions of followers are created by YouTubers who had a passion they wanted to share with an audience. To do the same, the first thing you must do is identify what your passions and talents are.

What's real and proven about creating a passion-based YouTube channel is that you cannot go wrong. Passion always drives success.

In the world of content creation, knowing how long and how much effort is required to grow a thriving channel, your passion is the fuel that will keep you going until things start to snowball. Consider this for a moment. Have you ever been given a task or project you disliked or didn't care about? Can you recall how laborious and lengthy the process was? Perhaps you ended up procrastinating, quit then un-quit several times over, and it was an experience you couldn't wait to finish.

Now think about a time when you got to work on a project you absolutely love. How enjoyable was that experienced?

You probably skipped meals, worked overtime including weekends, and even forgo your weekend Netflix Binge-watching just because of how immersed you were. When it comes to your YouTube content creation and channel management, it should feel more like the second example. How do you do this? Let me share a simple process to help you identify a topic you are passionate about. Once you pin that down and it feels right for you, every other choice will revolve around that passion.

How to discover your own passion and turn it into video content for YouTube.

Open up your Google docs or word document, and let's carry out an exercise to help you identify what you're passionate about. Remember, this exercise should be fun. Don't overthink things. Write anything and everything that comes to mind because there is no right or wrong. If nothing comes, make something up.

Step one: Ask yourself this question - What do I love doing and talking about?
Example answer: I love running in nature, cooking, traveling, reading comic books, painting, hiking, and writing poetry.

Step two: Answer this question - I can spend hours

reading, researching, thinking, and learning
about...X...[fill in your blank].

Example answer: I can spend hours reading,
researching, thinking, and learning about comic
books and creating my own characters.

Step three: Write down all the activities you've
enjoyed throughout your life. Go back as far as you
can and list everything down.

Example answer: Selling lemonade when I was
nine, drawing manga as a teen, playing piano, cooking, painting with watercolors, juggling, writing
comedy, etc. Anything and everything you've
enjoyed doing should go on this list whether you did
it a year ago or ten years ago.

Step four: Write down all your strengths, skills,
and any work experience you've had. Make sure
these are practical.

Example answer: social media manager, sales repre-
sentative, party planner, florist, etc.

Step five: What are some of your personality traits
that people say they like about you? Three qualities
that people have mentioned really make you unique.
They have to be positive traits, and if you don't

know, then text a few friends now and ask them to share with you.

Example answer: Funny, resilient, and confident.

Step six: Pick and choose, and then put in some research time.

Pick the top three topics or activities that stand out from your list and order them in priority. The one with the most electrifying energy is the one you should start researching most.

Researching in this context means you should head over to the YouTube search bar and start typing in the topics you've chosen. See what comes up. How much content has been created around your passion? Are people engaging, commenting, and liking existing content? What quality is the content? Which titles are performing best? Click on the channels with the content you're passionate about and notice how that channel is set up. If you'd like to see exact metrics and volume search, I recommend getting a Google Chrome extension like VidIQ or Keywords Everywhere. These are great for helping you figure out what keywords and content are performing well at high volume and low competition.

The purpose of doing research is to ensure you're going after an interest that has an existing and engaged audience. Most people say YouTube is oversaturated, and it's too late to start a channel. I disagree strongly. I think now is the best time to start your channel, and you can grow it even faster than the rest of us because you get to ride the wave of success we've already created.

By finding channels that are posting on the topic you're passionate about, you can get ideas of content topics that work. You also get to see the mistakes they are making or the gaps that still need to be filled. You will also feel what the audience cares about and what they want to see more of. So if you find competition around your topic, get excited because you're on the right path, and I will show you strategies to leverage this competition.

Now that you've identified your passion and validated that there's an audience for that topic, it's time to start thinking of content that you can post. If you've not yet identified what you love, don't worry. Here are some more questions that will help.

1. If you could be remembered for three things after you're gone from this life, what would you want those three to be?
2. If money wasn't an issue and you had financial freedom, what would you do with your time?
3. What is one thing your friends and family usually

come to you to ask for advice or a recommendation? Make sure it's something you also enjoy helping them out with.

FOR MONEY

Some people decide to start their YouTube channel because they hear of the many YouTubers making a full-time income and traveling the world. There are also countless stories of content creators that have started a side-hustle of YouTube content creation and ended up generating more passive income than their primary job salary.

For example, I have a friend who was employed as a customer service rep in a furniture company. He decided to test out his ability to succeed on YouTube and generate passive income by teaching arts and crafts, DIY sessions, and promoting unique furniture pieces. His channel now earns him about $15k in passive income each month, which is more than the salary he gets working at the store. So if you've been wondering how to make a side income or even if you want to be a full-time YouTuber traveling the world and creating amazing content of the cool places you're exploring, this can be a great way to fund that lifestyle.

Many consider YouTube to be the king of the side hustle. Why? Here are some of the reasons worth knowing if you want to increase your income.

- YouTube monetization is very consistent and can be very lucrative if you have the right strategy. In a later section, we will be talking about different ways to monetize. For now, realize that as a content creator on YouTube, you will have the opportunity to generate income on your channel.
- They're recurring and evergreen income possibilities on YouTube. What do I mean by this? You can create a video this week and three years from now still make money from it. After interviewing lots of YouTubers and plotting my own success on the platform, I noticed some similarities. A key one that stands out is that video creation has been going on for years for all of us. Years ago, when we started making the videos, no one knew us. Video views ranged from a few hundred to a few thousand if we were lucky, but we just kept creating awesome videos.

I can tell you, there was no income coming in at that point for any of us. I certainly never made a dime. But I kept persisting. After a few years, I noticed my growth started to gain momentum, and then slowly, a few thousand views turned into a few hundred thousand. By that time, the subscriber count was decent enough, and each video's earnings started adding up. Ultimately, a good steady income becomes a reality. This is pretty much what I've heard from almost every fellow creator I've interviewed, with just a few exceptions. All this to say, you can do it, but you need to play the long game. And the best part about YouTube is the more mature your channel becomes. The better you'll be rewarded by your older content as long as you didn't take shortcuts initially.

Suppose you're looking for a side hustle or want a lifestyle that's funded entirely by your content creation. In that case, I do think YouTube is excellent for helping you accomplish this. And as I shared with you, I know many people who earn more from their YouTube than their 9 to 5.

FOR FAME

Want to become YouTube famous? It's not too late, but you need to be prepared to put in the work.

Being YouTube famous has become a real thing. It is considered just as substantial as being a rock-star. Of course, it's not as easy as it used to be, but it's still possible.

If you want to become a social media influencer or grow a brand, YouTube is a great platform to help you create fame. Nowadays, some of the most famous YouTubers have the same special treatment as TV celebrities. Have you noticed? I have seen comedians, musicians, and other types of entertainers jumpstart their careers by being "discovered" on YouTube. Even Justin Beiber first started out on YouTube. So whether you want to grow a personal brand, a company brand, or become a well-known social media celebrity, YouTube has the potential to make that happen for you.

But before you get too excited, let's make sure you're setting realistic expectations. If you think YouTube will make you a celebrity overnight, you are sorely mistaken. There was a time when it could happen, but given how mature the platform has become, it will take a lot more strategic thinking and effort.

When YouTube first started, platform tools like the video response tool could be leveraged to gain a new audience's attention. You could piggyback on the rise and success of a YouTube star just by directly engaging on their hit videos using the video-response tool. This option no longer exists.

There's also the opportunity of collaborating with other successful YouTubers. That could help you get in front of a huge audience and go from zero to famous in a day, but unfortunately, a lot of work goes into creating these collaborations nowadays. There has to be a real-world connection. The more prominent stars are increasingly difficult to access if one is just getting started. Besides, just because someone has a big audience doesn't mean they will automatically subscribe to your channel. And then, of course, there is the growing issue of creating high-quality videos with graphics, great studio lighting, scenery, etc. Top creators already have the financing, resources, and support from the partner program and other sponsorships, but when you're just starting out, all you have a webcam in your bedroom or living room. It's going to take a while before people start to respect and admire what you do. But if you keep persisting, it is possible.

ACTIVITY #2: FINDING YOUR MOTIVATION

It's time to implement what you've just learned in this chapter.

If you want to become successful with your YouTube endeavor, you need to know what drives you. What is causing you to start this channel? What's your big "WHY" for this? The bigger the way, the more likely you are to persist and succeed. To do this, here are some questions to answer.

1. What is my goal for this YouTube channel?

2. Why am I choosing that goal as my primary goal?

3. How far am I willing to stretch to make the goal a reality?

4. What is my vision for myself if I think about where I want to be 2 years from now?

5. What is the vision for the channel? I.e., what do I want it to represent?

6. Why is the success of this channel so vital to me now?

7. How will my life change when I hit the goals I have set for this YouTube channel?

II

YOUR YOUTUBE CHANNEL

DETERMINE YOUR FOCUS

*a*s we start to gain momentum on this quest to becoming a highly successful income-producing YouTuber, it's time to turn your focus on delivering value. What can you bring to the platform that will cause others to pay attention, engage with your content, and become loyal subscribers? To help you answer that question effectively and efficiently, we will break down how you can pick or decide on a niche. I'll also share with you the best types of niches that are performing well. But before we get to that, perhaps you're wondering why picking a niche is essential.

I've found myself in heated conversations with smart business owners who wondered the same thing. Creatives struggle to understand that marketing to everyone means you're marketing to no one. Recently I was introduced to a life and health coach who was in the process of starting his

YouTube channel. He wants to become an authority on the platform and attract hot leads that can easily convert into paying customers, and he wants that to happen fast. When I asked what his niche would be, he hesitated and then said, *"I want to help billions of people, so I don't want to limit myself by being so narrow with a niche topic."*

That, my friend, is the recipe for YouTube failure, especially now that it has gained maturity. The best performing channels are super niched. And you know why? Because when you focus on one vertical, you become known as the industry leader, the credible resource, and the go-to person for that topic. When new potential subscribers and future buyers come across your content and immediately understand the problem you can solve for them, they are more likely to stick around, engage, connect, and convert. When you focus on one niche, you have clarity, and people love clarity. It also makes your channel more memorable. Can you imagine how Coca Cola would be if they had started years ago advertising soft drinks, shoes, and food? It would have been extra hard to build the fortified brand we've all grown accustomed to. Everyone sees that red label on a soft drink or that Santa holding a bottle, and we immediately think - Coca-Cola.

You don't have deep pockets and years of branding budget to waste, so please save yourself by focusing on a niche. Bring as much clarity and simplicity to your new audience as you can, so they quickly associate you with the result you offer.

PICKING A NICHE

How, then, does one determine a niche for their new channel? In the case of the life and health coach I mentioned above, he could talk about mindset, lifestyle, working out, healthy eating, nutrition, and the list goes on and on. While he can always create content around any of these major categories once his channel gains momentum, it is best to focus on one vertical when just starting out. But which one first?

You may be having a hard time determining your niche, or perhaps you have too many options available. Regardless, we can still help you figure out the perfect niche for you. To start, go back to the answers from previous chapters. The exercises you've been doing so far are a foundation for this particular exercise because now you understand a bit more about yourself and why you want this channel. Now it's time to dive deeper. We need to find that sweet spot between gained knowledge about yourself and what we know about your ideal audience. In other words, the overlap between what you love (what you're passionate about) and what your ideal audience wants is the sweet spot for your content. That becomes your niche topic.

SEVEN STEPS TO HONING DOWN YOUR NICHE

One. Review your strengths and skills

The first step is detailing the ways you've been most helpful to others throughout your career. If you're just coming out of college and think about what friends usually come to you for help with. Again, want you to write the answers down. What skills have you developed? What leading roles and responsibilities have you had? What primary benefits did you deliver in the roles you've had? What successes have you had? Make sure to be super specific here.

Two. Map out your ideal audience and what they need.

It's imperative to identify what your ideal audience consider valuable and what needs they have that you can fulfill. To better figure out this piece of the puzzle, you need to create a perfect audience persona profile. Here are some of the questions to answer for that persona profile.

- Whom would you love to work with?
- What shared values do you have with this person?
- What makes him or her unique?
- Why does this person come to YouTube? What is he/she looking to experience?

- What are his/her goals and ambitions?
- What is his/her current challenges and worries?
- What is his/her purchase behavior? For example, they research online but like to buy offline.
- What is a pain or problem or lack they are experiencing as it relates to what your channel can offer?

Three. Research to see if there's a demand for your identified topic.

Now that you've found that sweet spot between what you love and what your audience needs, it's time to head over to YouTube and see how much demand there is for your topic. We do this to make sure there are actual people out there who want to watch your content type. To effectively conduct this research, you need to write down some keywords from your chosen topic or some titles that you would make a video about. Then type in that title or those keywords on the YouTube search to see what comes up. If there's a ton of results (millions of results), then I suggest getting a bit more specific with that title. If there are zero results, then no one may be looking for that type of content. What I recommend is to create content that is somewhere in between those two extremes.

Four. Do some due diligence for income earning potential.

Just because a topic is popular doesn't mean it's right for you, especially if you're looking to get rich. Many niches do well on the platform but don't earn the content creator much money. So if you want to make a lot of money through your channel, make sure you check to see income earning potential. Find out if a company would be willing or likely to sponsor you to use their products or whether you can create a side business alongside your channel. Monetization is worth thinking about before settling on a niche. Sponsorship is very lucrative when done right, but you need a good strategy; otherwise, it won't work. Your channel must be aligned with the income avenue you wish to leverage most. For example, if you want to be paid by brands, then definitely research the brands that seem to be paying fellow YouTubers to create content. Most good creators always let their audience know when doing sponsored content, so that's a great way of getting some companies' names within your niche. If you're interested in sponsorship, then make sure you have some offers to give to your audience as they learn to trust you. Having this plan from the start ensures you'll make all the right choices, including niche picking.

BEST TYPES OF YOUTUBE NICHES

Not every niche can be monetized. The most popular ones do work well, and some are way easier than others. Here's a list of the most popular and easy to monetize niches.

How-to tutorials

I personally think this is the most popular and best niche to get into on YouTube. Based on my experience, most people who come into this platform are looking to learn something. And since we all at some point need to know something, starting a channel that teaches "how-to" for your skill, talent or passion seems like a great idea. It can also become very lucrative. Answering "how to..." questions can quickly build your audience and generate clients for your brand or business. Whether it's how to tie your unique shoelaces, how to clean your carpets, how to make certain floral arrangements for a particular occasion, how to get rid of a stain, or whatever else you do, you could easily gather tens of thousands if not millions of views over time.

Animals

Cute animals have been trending on YouTube since the beginning, and the trend hasn't slowed down. This niche is still popular, and given how trendy cat videos have become, you can consider getting into this niche if you love animals.

That doesn't mean everyone with cats should start a YouTube channel. Make sure it aligns with your brand and the objective of the channel. For example, a bakery should not get into this niche! A vet should definitely consider having a channel around cute animals. You can create content with animals doing funny things and centre it on humor and entertainment. If you're more of the educational type, consider making videos on animal training, pet product reviews, and even animal care.

Lifestyle

Lifestyle has become one of the more popular niches on the platform. I think it's mainly due to the fact that a lifestyle vlogger doesn't neatly fit into any particular niche. So their content can be wildly varied and carry differing undertones. Some lifestyle vloggers rely heavily on humor, sarcasm, drama, or gossip, which gives their content that extra edge that people seem to love. Another thing about lifestyle vlogging is that it's incredibly personal. People usually disclose a lot of personal information about themselves, so if you tend to lead a private life, perhaps this wouldn't be the right type of content for you.

Food

Cooking and all things food-related are huge on YouTube. So if you love to cook or eat and critique food, you can create a successful channel with a vast audience. Show off amazing recipes, share some of the gadgets and tools you use in the kitchen, and you can't go wrong. Foodies are abundant on YouTube.

Gaming

I think the most famous YouTubers are gamers. Someone correct me if I'm wrong, but some of these individuals have become real-world celebrities. PewDiePie, Jack Septiceye, Markiplier, SSSniperWolf are just a few names that have gained global recognition. Why? Because these individuals have dominated YouTube. They are making tons of money doing what they love the most - gaming. You could be the same, but of course, you need to be fresh and different.

Makeup

One of the most popular YouTube niches is makeup, so if you're in the beauty space, this is a great starting point. And before you assume I am only talking about women's makeup, I'd like to point out that you could do really well with men's makeup. Yes, you read me right. Even men want tutorials around how to do their makeup! Be forewarned, though; competition is fierce with this niche, but the audience pretty huge and engaged.

Fashion

Fashion is another popular niche on YouTube, and you can approach it from various angles even if you're not a designer. You can review clothing items, share styling tips, or, if you're talented, start your own fashion line. This is one of the best and easier niches to get sponsors or even do affiliate marketing, which we will delve into later on.

Tech review

As we become a more tech-driven society, more and more people are coming to YouTube to watch tutorials or reviews on the latest tech and software products. Whether it's apps and software or physical hardware, you will have an audience if you can create engaging and valuable content. Are you good at helping others learn how to operate, assemble, or choose the right tech for their needs?

You can focus on workplace and productivity tech, home tech, or even small tech gadgets that we carry around our pockets daily. Your only limitation is your lack of imagination and creativity.

Sports

Are you a sport fantastic or maybe a former pro or amateur athlete? Then YouTube has an audience that would love your content. I have seen everything from sports vloggers to amateur reporters following around their favorite sports teams and sharing a different perspective with their audience than what professional journalists would share. And all of these types of content do really well. You don't have to be an officially appointed ambassador to create awesome content and keep your audience updated with the latest news. All you need is passion. Just be careful not to show copyrighted materials because that would lead to many unpleasant experiences with the authorities.

Photography

Another popular niche is photography. Many budding photographers look to YouTube for good advice on how to take better shots. You can offer tutorials on photography itself and also on the equipment that you use. This can be a great channel for affiliate marketing opportunities.

Travel

Who doesn't love a great travel channel? Some of the sexiest YouTube channels that I've come across are travel channels with great storytelling infused into them. There is a huge and very hungry audience waiting for you if you love to travel the world and have cool stories to share. People love to escape their current reality or that horrid cubicle with a good travel video. It inspires, motivates, and uplifts travel enthusiasts. The best part is many full-time YouTubers are also digital nomads traveling the world and finding creative ways to cover their expenses so they can continue to build their channel. If your dream is to travel the world, YouTube could be your golden ticket to seeing some of the best-hidden gems and the richest cultures our planet has to offer.

Music

Do you have a passion for music? Do you compose, sing, DJ, review, or teach others how to play an instrument? YouTube is an excellent platform for launching yourself. Some of the most viewed videos are music videos, and the best part is that you can go into any music genre and you'll still get a decent audience size. I also know some channels that do commentaries on music news, give advice, report on the latest news from their favorite musicians, or even teach others how to play a particular instrument. Your options are endless when it comes to content types, and there's a healthy audience to support you.

ASMR

ASMR or Autonomous Sensory Meridian Response has really grown in the last few years. It's all about the experience - using soothing sounds and imagery to relax viewers. ASMR content creators are all about taking their audience on a transformative journey through their sense organs.

And there you have it: the top niches on YouTube that are not only popular, but also easier to monetize. These niches already have audiences looking for content daily, so if you happen to pick one of these, you are in luck. There's a ready-made audience for you, thanks to the work of your peers who launched before you. All you have to do is develop the right plan to attract some of those engaged people to your channel.

ACTIVITY #3: TIME TO CHOOSE

As you might have realized by now, each chapter has to close with an implementation step. After having gone through the different exercises and discovered the top-performing niches, it's time to pick your niche.

Review your notes and come up with the top three niches that excite you the most. If you already know precisely the one to go for, that's great. But I encourage you to have more than one that you can start experimenting with for at least six weeks before settling on one. This is because I have seen many of my students get bored a few weeks into their content creation and give up on growing their channel. Listen, you'll need to consistently create unique content for the next many years if you want to succeed at this. Therefore you need to pick a niche that you are confident won't become a bore or burden 50 videos into it. That's why to get started I suggest having more than one - but limited to three -different verticals and then creating content on each for a short while to see which one still excites you after a few weeks. It also gives you the chance to see what the audience response is so you can test if one of them attracts more eyeballs and subscribers.

Pro tip:

When you make your choice, be sure to pick complementary niches. For example, Lifestyle vlogging and photography can align well. If, after a few weeks, you realize lifestyle isn't for you, then it's perfectly fine to focus on photography only. Now it's your turn. What niche will you choose?

4

UNDERSTANDING YOUR AUDIENCE

*T*here are a lot of unhelpful myths surrounding the existing YouTube audience. It will serve you well to read and understand this chapter carefully as it will impact your content strategy and channel growth moving forward.

Most people assume YouTube is for young single male personas or that only the younger demographics are active users. This is actually not accurate. According to a study conducted by Google and Nielsen, the average YouTube viewer is just as likely to be female as male. And this thing about young single Millenials being the only audience is also a myth because the same research said YouTube users are more likely to have kids compared to non-users.

Another report, by Cast from Clay, shared U.S. statistics around YouTube users and revealed data that proved men and women use YouTube equally. There's a robust usage of the platform across all age groups, so this isn't just a younger demographic platform like TikTok and others. You will find a healthy and active audience of 65-75-year-olds. Granted, they don't use the platform in the same proportions are the 15-30-year-olds. Still, they are actively engaged nonetheless. The data from Cast from Clay shows 96% users aged between 18 - 24 years, 95% users aged between 25 - 34 years old, 90% users aged between 35 - 44 years old, 85% users ages between 45 - 54 years old, 79% of users aged between 55 - 64 years old, 66% aged between 65 - 75 years old and 51% users aged 75 and over. Keep in mind these statistics reflect US users only. What we can take away from this is that there are all kinds of YouTube users ranging from teenagers to retired. Even in the United Kingdom, the statistics remain steady, showing YouTube has a stronghold in every age group and demographic.

How does knowing these different types of YouTube viewers benefit you?

It's very simple. You can have any kind of channel you desire, and your ideal audience will be ready to embrace your brand. Remember, you cannot become a video influencer if there's no one to influence. Well, I have just proven to you that on YouTube, you can become an influencer at any age, for any demographic. The most important thing is to figure out what audience your content will serve and then focus on understanding what your people want. It's not enough to create a persona based on shallow things like gender, location, age, and job title. You need to know your audience more deeply so they can immediately resonate with your channel.

UNDERSTANDING YOUR COMPETITION

If you're a beginner, this part will help you quickly determine what works and what doesn't in your niche. It will also show you best practices, industry standards, and some benchmarks you can use to create an amazing channel. Even if you've got your channel set up, I still encourage you to pay attention to this section of the book. It's where you can learn how to check existing and trending channels in your niche. The goal isn't to copy your competition but to learn from them and improve upon what they've done. That way, your young channel can shave off some of the mistakes and learning curves they had to go through. Let's walk through how to do this now.

CREATING A BENCHMARK FOR YOUR CHANNEL

Make sure to fire up your Google doc or Word document so you can create your own custom benchmark in this process. Make sure to document this as much as possible.

Step one: Find the best performing channels in your niche.

I recommend gathering the top five to ten preferred channels where you know your audience is hanging out. Not sure how to find your competition? Here's a simple exercise.

Do in-depth market research online to figure out who is talking about the same topic or selling the same products and services you want to sell. By now, you should have the primary keyword or niche topic that you'll be focusing on. Take that keyword or keyphrase and start by putting it on the main Google search bar to see what comes up. You'll see a list of websites and ads that are ranking for it, and if you click on the "video" tabs, you will see all the videos that are ranking on Google. This is great because it already shows you the channels competing with you. Record everything on your Google sheet and click the channels of these videos whenever one resonates with you so you can see how they've set up their entire YouTube channel.

You can also go to a software called Ubersuggest and type in each of the keywords. You'll get a downloadable report of all the websites ranking for that topic. Take the names of those sites and head over to the YouTube search bar to see what kind of content they have on their channel. If you realize some of these high-ranking websites don't have a great YouTube channel, then that's great because that's the opportunity you need to seize. If you find a great channel with lots of engagement and high-quality content, add that to your list of competitors. You can also do the same thing on other social media channels like Twitter and Instagram, especially if your topic is popular on these other networks. Just use hashtags to find the most engaged accounts and then spy on their YouTube channels. Your goal is to have a comprehensive list of between five to ten competitors. Then move on to the next step.

Step two: Take note of the following metrics for all the identified competitive YouTube channels.

- The Total Number of Subscribers on the Channel.
- Subscribers Change.
- The Total Number of Videos on the Entire Channel.
- Videos Change.
- Videos Table.
- Views Total.

- Views Change.
- View Subscriber Rate.
- Average Views Per Video.
- Engagement Rate.
- Average Engagement Per Video.
- Average Favorites Per Video.
- Average Likes Per Video.
- Average Dislikes Per Video.
- Average Comments Per Video.

Granted, this will be a lot of manual work, especially if your competitors have created lots of video content on their channel. So if you'd like a little bit of help with this process, consider using software such as SocialBlade, which is a free online tool that can help you track YouTube statistics more effortlessly. In the resources section, you will find all the tools I've recommended throughout this book.

Once you've gathered all this data, it's time to decide which benchmarks you will set for your channel. Allow that to influence the KPI's that you'll set in the coming months as well. How will you know if your channel is doing well?

The data collected from channels in your niche can help you figure out what a good audience engagement should be. You can continue using analytics to track growth month over month. Many of those basic data sets you will find in the

YouTube analytics dashboard. However, if you'd like something more robust to help you with analytics, consider investing in tools such as Tubular Intelligence, which allows you to see what's trending on YouTube as well as how your videos are performing. You can also get BuzzSumo, which is quite popular nowadays and has a YouTube Analyzer. This tool can help you find the right keywords, get a list of the most popular videos for your niche, analyze specific videos, or keep an eye on competitor channels.

Find my audience Tool

This is a new tool by "Think With Google" that I've played around with and found it extremely useful. It will help you get an overview of where your audience might be hanging out on YouTube, which channels they are likely watching, and what they might plan to buy.

Once on the site (www.thinkwithgoogle.com/feature/find-myaudience), you can begin by taking a tour. There's a "Take a tour" tab on the top right corner, which walks you through how the site works. I recommend signing in with your Gmail so you can save the detailed information you gather. For example, I typed in "In-market" for my audience preference, and then chose the category of sports and fitness. With that, I learned that there are three YouTube audiences who are researching or planning to purchase sports and fitness related products or services. The three groups are fitness products and services, outdoor recreational equipment, and sporting goods. When I clicked on fitness products and services, I found the top YouTube channels people shopping for fitness products and services are likely to be watching. Jeff Nippard (2.14M), Body project (1M+), Sydney Cummings (706K), Muscle & Strength (816K) are the channel names that popped up.

The tool also revealed some of the top products and services most relevant to my audience, including Activewear, video games, etc. This is valuable information for someone setting up his or her fitness channel, wouldn't you agree?

Now you can have access to the same so that your channel can reach the right audience with the right message and offers based on their preferences.

ACTIVITY #4: THE CHANNELS ON YOUR CHOSEN NICHE

It's time to implement all that we've learned. In this activity, you will complete researching between five to ten competitor channels using the tools I suggested.

- Identify what makes these channels popular.
- Identify some of the gaps, if any, or think of what you could do differently and better.

- Read as many comments as possible so you can see how the channel interacts with their audience. This is also a great opportunity to gain content ideas because you will find questions, concerns, or even requests from the community that you can leverage on your own channel.

- Record as many of the detailed metrics I shared earlier as you can. If you do it manually, then do the best you can. Otherwise, use tools like Social Blade, BuzzSumo, and Tubular Intelligence. Once you've done this extensive research, start looking for the gaps in content and brainstorm how you can improve on what you've seen out there. Document every idea, no matter how trivial it may seem. These notes will come in handy as we get into strategy and implementation.

BRANDING YOUR CHANNEL

It's time to get to the fun and creative part of setting up your channel. Now that you know what your channel will be about and whom you'll be creating content for, we need to create the different graphics, artworks, and other necessary pieces so that your channel can instantly attract potential subscribers. That's where branding comes in.

WHY YOU NEED TO BRAND

You'll find different definitions of what a brand is in today's digital world. I want to keep things super simple, so here's how we will approach this branding concept.

Branding is about taking the best aspects of you and recreating them online so that people can have a real sense of who you are and what you stand for the moment they land on your YouTube channel. It's a lot harder to make a great first impression online, so by giving your channel an identity that's true to you, there's a higher chance you'll bridge that gap better and use technology to reinforce relationships rather than hinder.

Branding has become extremely important on YouTube because you need to stand out and attract the right attention from the right people. Social media has also become very dominated by alluring aesthetics. Like it or not, if your channel doesn't look appealing to the audience you wish to attract, it will be tough gaining momentum. Most importantly, I emphasize branding a lot on YouTube because it is a social platform built around the concept of community at the end of the day and sharing knowledge and ideas. That means there's a strong need for s sense of belonging for the people hanging out there. Your branding does wonders when it comes to creating a signpost with your core identity written all over it, and that helps your "tribe" recognize and connect with you.

How do you go about establishing your brand?

That cannot be rushed. It is a natural growth process that will get better as you create content and interact with community members. However, a few key questions will enable us to start the journey of branding your YouTube channel. Ask yourself the following:

- Who am I, and how do I want to be known on YouTube? For example, a speaker, digital marketer, life coach, etc.
- What kind of voice do I want to build on YouTube? For example, funky, laid back, humorous, formal, etc.
- What kind of vocabulary, personality, and verbiage will I use? For example, think of Gary Vee. His language and vocabulary are very distinct. You want to figure out what yours is.
- What emotions, experience, and benefit do you want your tribe to have as a result of consuming your content?
- What colors and design will you be using to stand out?

These are just a handful of questions you will need to answer as you build your brand. In this chapter, I will walk you through the key elements and how to set each one up. Follow along, and by the end of this, you will have your channel ready for launch.

SETTING UP YOUR NEW YOUTUBE CHANNEL

If you already have a channel set up, you may skip this section if you like, but I still encourage you to go through it. To get started, you first need to sign up for a Gmail account. If you already have an account with Google, then head over to youtube.com and click on the Sign In button on the top right corner.

If you're creating the account for the first time, you will be asked to choose whether you're creating a channel for yourself or a business once you sign up. You will have the option of creating a personal brand or business brand, depending on your objective.

You will need to fill out the details such as your name, the name you want to use for the channel, and then choose to verify the account. Later on, you can also choose to add a channel manager if you've set up a business channel. To verify your channel, you will need to give a mobile number where a text or voice message will be sent with a code. Once the code is entered and accepted, YouTube will let you upload videos longer than 15 minutes, add custom thumbnails, do Livestream, and so much more. So please make sure you do this as fast as possible.

Once this is done, you can head over to your channel dashboard, and you'll see a blank canvas for you to add your creativity and personality to. This is where the fun begins. If you have other social media profiles or websites you'd like to add to the main dashboard, you can add them here. For now, the most essential step is to add the artworks and graphics that will personalize your channel and make it more appealing to your ideal audience.

Channel Images

Let's pick out the main image elements for your channel. Even if you're not a design expert, you can still create incredible images without spending a fortune or hiring expensive graphics designers. Tools such as Canva, PicMonkey, Word Swagg, Picktochart are just a few of the tools you need to add to your toolbox. These software products are either free or low cost and require little to no experience in graphics design. My preferred is, of course, Canva, which has a free and pro version. With Canva, you can design epic looking images in a matter of seconds, from your channel art and logo to your thumbnails, and so on.

Hire a professional to create your graphics.

You can also hire a professional to create your channel art if you have a little budget to spare. Websites such as 99designs are great for outsourcing, but you can also go to Upwork or

Fiverr and hire someone for as little as $5 as long as you know exactly what you want.

Once you have the main channel image, it's time to brand your new channel. Here's how:

Sign in to your YouTube studio and from the left menu select Customization. Use the tabs to customize your channel by changing the profile picture, banner image, and video watermark. This is also where you'll have the ability to change the layout.

For the profile picture, YouTube recommends uploading a JPG, GIF, BMP, or PNG file of 800 X 800 px. It can be square or round that renders at 98 X 98 px. Don't use animated GIFs for this.

For the banner image, you need a minimum dimension of 2048 X 1152 px, with an aspect ratio of 16:9. The file size must be 6MB or smaller. If you go with the minimum recommended dimensions, make sure that the area for text and logos is 1235 X 338 px. Larger images may get cropped on specific devices because the banner comes across differently depending on whether it's being viewed on desktop, mobile, or TV displays.

For basic channel info, you also can personalize what is displayed by adding or removing the information you want to be shared with the public. If you want to have a different name from your Google Account, you will need to create a brand account. This would be different from your personal Google Account, and it will make it easier to give other people (team members) access to your YouTube channel without sharing your Google Account details. It's also great if you know you'll want to have multiple channels in one account. For influencers, I highly recommend getting a Brand Account because of the flexibility it offers. The best part is, you get to call your channel whatever name you like.

Channel Layout

You can customize your channel so that new viewers and potential subscribers can see your channel trailers, certain featured sections, or a featured video when they first land on your homepage. Channel trailers are great because they offer the new visitor a preview of your channel and what you're all about. It's a great way to make a positive first impression and really connect with your audience. Setting up a trailer video is easy. Just select Customization and then "Layout." Once you see "Video spotlight," click ADD and select the video that you want to make the trailer. Hit publish and you'll have your very own trailer. Making a great video trailer is important, so keep reading to learn how to create an epic video that leaves your audience wanting more.

If you don't want to have a trailer for the homepage, you could also feature a particular video. Some YouTubers place their most-watched video as the first thing a new visitor sees so they can immediately receive value and see why everyone else has subscribed to that channel. So don't feel pressured to create a trailer; even a high-value content piece will work just as well.

ACTIVITY #5: CREATE YOUR CHANNEL

Now that you have all the basic elements of setting up your channel, it's time to implement what you've learned. Before you get into the next chapter, I want you to decide what kind of a channel you want to set up and then get to work coming up with the design, image profile, and logo if necessary. Then head over to YouTube and create your channel. Feel free to explore the different menus in YouTube Studio and also read the community guidelines they offer. Section four of this book will cover more on how to navigate YouTube Studio, but I don't want you to wait. Create your channel now.

III

CREATING YOUTUBE
VIDEOS

6

CREATING QUALITY CONTENT

*T*his section of our book focuses purely on creating amazing content that will get you views and subscribers. For creatives, this is probably the most exciting part of their YouTube channel management. But why invest time learning how to create quality content?

- Your content will stand out more if it's of better quality than your competitors.
- Quality content is usually so packed with value that a new audience can't help but want more of what you're creating, which will lead to more subscribers.
- With great content comes the potential of going viral.
- Quality content will serve you for years to come.

We call it evergreen content only because once you create it, the number of views, engagement, and potential business grows overtime. I have a video that's three years old and still brings in new business inquiries.

WHAT EXACTLY IS QUALITY CONTENT?

Simply stated, quality refers to the experience of the user. You can have lots of bells and whistles on your video, but if the users have a poor experience, then it won't matter. That content will be considered a flop. Quality includes all the technical aspects of video, including audio quality, visual quality, editing quality, and the quality of the actual script or content being shared. For example, you need to think about whether the video will be HD or 4K. Then, ask yourself, are the colors, right? Is the lighting, right? Is it sharp and crisp? Is the audio good? Was it edited in a way that makes sense and tells a story? These are a few examples of objective quality, and the best part is that they are measurable and easy to control on your part.

However, we also need to think about subjective quality. This is what we really care about as human beings, and it will directly influence your channels' growth. It includes things like making it relevant, interesting, and engaging to the end-user.

According to a Google report, "when people are choosing what to watch, relating to their passions is 1.6X more important than whether the content has high production quality." [Source: Google and OMG, U.S., "Personal Prime-time" Study, n=3,200 respondents, Oct.2018. I'm sharing this with you to let you know that both objective and subjective quality matter. And while the objective is easy to measure and control, the emotional quality will ultimately determine how well your channel does in the long run. We want to make sure you have the best chance of winning the hearts and attention of your potential subscribers. The best way to do that is to combine the technical aspects of video production with world-class content that resonates with the targeted audience. You need to come across as relatable, and the stuff you put out should be focused on providing value in some way, shape, or form—more on how to do that in the unfolding chapters.

THE DIFFERENT KINDS OF VIDEO CONTENT

Growing your YouTube channel does not have to be daunting or complicated. You just need to know which types of content people love to watch and create more of those types. Here are the top ones.

- How-to and Tutorials
- Behind-the-scenes video content.
- Interview and Q&A
- Pranks
- Vlog
- Product reviews
- 360
- User-generated content
- Webinar
- Presentation
- Livestream

How-to and Tutorials

Most of the famous YouTubers you might know have gotten that rise to stardom through this category of content. Millennials are exceptional at creating this type of video content. It performs well because people love watching videos, and they absolutely love watching actionable insights. When I say stardom - I mean serious riches and stardom. Some YouTubers have gone from zero to earning over $50 million just by creating awesome tutorials.

I love this type of content because you're not limited by anything, and you can be as creative as you want. As long as you understand your audience's values and create lots and lots of free content around it, you can't go wrong. It can be tutorials on anything under the sun. This is the age of information, and people love to learn. Just make sure the tutorials are actually high quality with the intention of helping, not making a sale!

Behind-the-scenes video content

These types of videos are great for companies and for solopreneurs. They are firmly rooted in raw storytelling for branding purposes. What do I mean by that? It's about revealing what you stand for, the culture you're building as a team or organization, and it pulls back the curtain on your brand to allow customers and potential buyers to forge a connection with your brand. It goes from being an impersonal operation to real human beings with emotions, frustrations, ambitions, and personalities. If you have a remote team, get creative about how to record and edit funny behind-the-scenes content. If you fly solo, perhaps you can show a behind-the-scenes or sneak peek video about an upcoming project. A great example of this type of content can be found on Mind Valley Academy or even Vistaprint.

Interview and Q&A

These types of video content are great for authority building. Suppose you can get influences, experts, or even celebrities to come and answer your questions. In that case, you'll start to attract the attention of the people who resonate with that information. This type of video content allows you to connect with and align your brand with inspiring people and thought leaders. It also helps you look more trustworthy since you're hanging out with and getting answers from a respected voice.

A good interview requires planning ahead but don't make it come across as too polished and scripted out. It should be natural and intimate so your potential subscribers can fuller immerse themselves in that experience and come out feeling like they know you and your guest better. As the interviewer, you need to ask powerful questions, direct the interview in the best direction, and make it as meaningful as possible for the user. I love interviews because you can create lots of evergreen content and never run out of ideas or topics. You can even give exclusive access to your audience if you can tap into well-known influencers and celebrities. There's a lot of power in leveraging this if you know how to do it right. A great example is Lewis Howes's "School of Greatness."

Pranks

There's a huge and hungry audience waiting for you on YouTube if you enjoy pulling off pranks. These types of video content are mostly for entertainment. As the creator, you would either prank a friend or stranger and capture it on film. Of course, you need to make sure the pranks are subtle enough to avoid offending anyone. What you're looking for is to make people laugh and disrupt their day or their thought patterns. Some people have been extreme and created a lot of controversies, and it seems to have worked. Still, I strongly urge you to avoid that because, based on what I've seen, people enjoy funny pranks, not offensive or extreme pranks.

Vlog

These are video blogs. They are usually raw and require minimal cost production. All you need is a unique brand voice and a personality that resonates with your target audience. Most vlogs are off-the-cuff and unpolished. All you need is a smartphone or webcam as equipment. I encourage you to have some kind of a script or bullet point to ensure your content is concise and well thought out. As a video influencer, you could do daily vlogs sharing your day at work. Think of this as documenting your journey. Whatever you're in the trenches trying to build, share it with the community, and you'll start to see a tribe joining you on the ride. I suggest checking out Gary Vaynerchuck's "Daily Vee" for inspiration on this type of video content.

Product Reviews

This type of video content is similar to how-to content. It's meant to be insightful and focused on helping, not selling a product. Consumers flock to YouTube every minute of the hour, looking for help along their purchase journey. They want to know which product is best, how it works, and whether it will be good value for their money. A product review can help answer all those questions. However, I would recommend doing product reviews once you've established some credibility and trust with your audience because they need to trust you before following your advice. Affiliate marketing partners up very well with product review videos. But again, you will need to walk that fine line of helping your audience make the right decision, not just selling them something because you're making money. By the way, you don't even need to talk about products in your niche. For example, if you're a personal trainer, you could talk about the best running shoes or home workout equipment - even if they aren't directly related to you. Bringing that level of service and customer-focused value to an audience can cause someone to trust you and even end up hiring your personal training services. Think creatively about which products you review and have the intention of bringing value.

360 or VR content

360 degrees videos are the latest alternatives we have as we move closer toward a full virtual experience. Yes, we still have a long way to go, but people dig 360 content as it is immersive and puts the users in the centre of the action

allowing them to pan around the room with their smart device. In other words, this type of content focuses more on bringing an immersive and exciting experience to the end-user. Don't think you need to be fancy or have a huge company to make these types of videos work for you. Experiment and see if it matches your brand and personality.

User-generated content

This type of video content will work once you have a growing customer base. If you have an existing business, then find creative ways to get previous or existing customers to create social content. Something sharable that sells for you. User-generated content has become massive on social media. It's a great way to get free testimonials, demonstrate your credibility, and gather new leads because people love to see social proof. Most social media users say that UGC is the most authentic type of content, and they want to see more of it. So whether you're just starting out and need time to build a customer list or already have people who can create this for you, come up with a plan and incentive to make people want to record short videos talking about how great your brand is. Wondering how to get started? Consider running a contest on YouTube and other social media platforms. Encourage people to send over videos of themselves using your product. Or you can start a campaign for your brand and products and create a trending hashtag, then ask people to use it as much as possible.

Webinar

Did you know you could host webinars on Google hangout? It's simple and easy to navigate. This type of video content is extremely valuable for an audience that loves to learn. It can exponentially grow your YouTube channel because you can offer webinars and share them on your channel. Just make sure it's educative and actionable information. Since the pandemic in 2020, we've seen a massive spike in virtual webinars, so now people are accustomed to learning online. If you don't want to use Google Hangouts, you can do Zoom webinars and then upload the recording to your YouTube channel. Think of webinars as a free live event. An opportunity for your potential subscribers to learn something valuable from you and begin the purchase journey as well. It can be a solo webinar, or you could invite a roundtable panel discussion with several gurus in your niche.

Presentations

Ever heard of Ted Talks? Of course, you have! These are a form of presentation content, and as you know, they perform really well on YouTube. A presentation type of video content (even if it's not a Ted Talk) can work really well because it combines the excitement of a live event with a virtual webinar's practicality to create something compelling and shareable. You could be on the other side of the planet watching a presentation from someone you could have never met. Of course, if you want to do Ted Talks, you can do that too, but I think there's a long process of making that happen. If you're going to leverage this type of video content, I encourage you to start by giving as many presentations as possible at different locations. The size of the audience doesn't matter. Just make sure the presentation itself is excellent and that you capture the whole thing on video.

Livestreaming

The last type of video content we will discuss is Live streaming, which was added a few years ago. Since then, there has been increasing demand across all social platforms, including YouTube. People love interacting in a Livestream, and it is expected to become a $70.5 billion industry by 2021. YouTube gives you the ability to participate and enjoy a portion of that success. The best part about live streaming is that you can do it on any category, niche, and subject matter. Niches such as cooking, self-improvement, motivational speeches, DIY arts and crafts, makeup routines, dance choreography, workout routines, yoga, meditation, etc. can all perform great on the Live stream.

Why does this work so well? It comes down to the fact that people love the suspense of Live video. They can't resist the urge to tune in because they don't want to miss out on getting new gossip, learning something new, or connecting with someone they admire.

Studies have shown that live streams generate up to 10X more engagement than regular videos. Neil Patel said that live video broadcasts receive 600% more engagement than regular posts. So what are you waiting for?

You can be completely unknown today, but if you create great content, you can become a YouTube superstar in no time using any of these content types.

WHY YOU NEED A SOLID VIDEO CONTENT STRATEGY

Creating a well thought out video content strategy is a must if you want long-term success. Here's the thing. It will take time to build up brand authority or a robust library that keeps drawing in traffic. That's okay. Instead of fussing about the daunting work ahead of you, focus on creating a simple and easy to execute system that you can follow. Ensure the plan you create is also flexible because you'll need to adjust things as you grow.

Why do you need to come up with a clear strategy? Because if you don't, you're going to end up disheartened and feeling like you're not making any progress. That will likely cause you to give up too soon. It's also going to be really hard to measure and monitor your growth if everything is random. Posting a piece of content idea that comes to you every once in a while will not bring you the growth you need. Trust me on that. And more importantly, I want to help ensure you never run dry of content ideas. The more precise and well planned out your strategy, the easier it will be to keep producing even when you go through a dry spell.

So how do we go about creating your strategy? I borrowed some insights from Think With Google, who share many relevant ideas on winning big on YouTube. They interview and run case studies on some of the biggest brands in the world. Think Johnson & Johnson, Nike, and even Marvel Movies. It's only wise to listen to the advice they have to offer on how to approach building fantastic content on our YouTube channels. We may not have the resources or money to create at the level of these giant corporations. Still, we can implement the same principles driving their success. A simple framework I have learned from my time studying those case studies is to Create + Collaborate + Curate.

THE 3 C'S FOR A SIMPLE AND EFFICIENT CONTENT STRATEGY

Create

Your strategy should include a detailed brainstorm of the titles, keywords, lessons, or subject matter your videos will cover over a certain period of time. We can call this a video content plan. For this section of your strategy, you will need to research the top-performing content in your niche market and then make a list of what you will create.

You can have a monthly content plan or a 90-day content plan depending on your preference. I recommend starting with a 30-day content plan to avoid overwhelm. Then decide whether you'll batch these videos together, so you shoot once or twice a week. If you're bold and committed to being on camera a lot, you can also shoot, edit, and publish on the same day. I recommend giving yourself enough leeway for any emergencies, equipment glitches, and even enough editing time.

If you plan on releasing one new video daily, the above options can all work well. If you're releasing more than one video a day, then you definitely need to batch your video recordings to allow ample editing and personalization time. Remember, the quantity must not compromise the quality of your video content.

Collaborate

The best way to build up your library and grow your brand on YouTube is to create strategic partnerships. There should be a section on your content strategy for collaborations with peers and other YouTube influencers. The great benefit of partnering up with others in your space is the increased exposure your channel gets.

Make sure, however, that the agreement is mutually beneficial. I would recommend creating an outreach campaign once you've hit your first 1K subscribers. And when you do, begin with those most likely to agree to this partnership. For example, asking someone with 3 million subscribers to collaborate with you when you only have 1K followers may not yield any positive results. Unless you're willing to pay them handsomely, these categories of YouTubers will be out of reach at first. But if you started reaching out to influencers with between 5K - 30K subscribers, they are more likely to want to work with you as long as you can prove how valuable the experience will be.

When you collaborate, you co-create the video content and then cross-post on each other's channels for maximum exposure. Not only will you be adding to your library, but you'll also bring value to a new audience that didn't know you existed.

For example, there's a YouTuber with a channel on physics experiments and how to apply it to everyday life. She collaborated with a guy who has a channel purely for testing out and reviewing tech gear. Their collaboration involved using physics to see whether the iPhone 11 Pro could withstand a massive hit without breaking. The video was entertaining and cool to watch, plus we learned a lot about Vacuum and how powerful nature is. Even the iPhone isn't built to withstand the powers of Mother Nature. I share this simple example to show you what's possible with collaborations. You can find the video on both channels, and now, the tech-savvy geeks who didn't know about the physics channel got a chance to subscribe and follow "Physics Girl." That's the power of a good collaboration.

Curate

The last C we want to add to your content strategy is one that involves curating content. This isn't content you create. Instead, it comes from existing customers, subscribers, and loyal fans that want to praise you and your brand. That's why this part of your content comes when the channels begin to mature because it's likely you're starting from scratch, and that's okay. Just know that you will be able to do this type of content at some point, and it'll really boost your credibility and authority. Fans and customers love sharing their experiences, stories, and opinions. Getting this type of content won't be too hard, especially if you're regularly running contests and giveaways. Think of it as a way to invite your audience to help you tell your story on YouTube.

A content strategy doesn't need to be perfect, but you must have one. With these three different areas, you also want to know what metrics and measurements of growth you'll be going after. As a beginner, here's a simple template I would encourage you to follow.

- Write down the big goals and the little goals that lead up to that big one.
- Write down whom the content is for.
- Write down the influencers your audience follows on YouTube.
- Write down the experience you want the audience to have and how the content should impact them.
- Write down the expected milestones and principal return on investment (ROI) that you expect.

HOW TO PLAN AHEAD WITH YOUR CONTENT

The more thought you put into your video content before hitting that record button, the better the quality and performance. Whether you're doing a technical how-to or a daily vlog, it's essential to plan ahead. How much planning you do is entirely up to you. Some people want to script out every word. Others need to have a vague idea of the main message they want to pass on before shooting. There's no wrong or right here. Your personality and experience with being on camera does influence how you will plan your video content. Still, I will share a few best practices below.

Keep in mind that the first place to start, as stated earlier, is with a documented content plan. It can be two weeks, thirty days, sixty days, or even a ninety-day plan. If you're one of those who cannot start thinking too far ahead, then opt for a weekly program. Sit with your journal or a Google document and plan out the video content topic, title, and key points you'll create over the specified period. You can also use a content calendar for this. If you approach your content planning from the perspective of creating a viral video or a single piece of content that will make you an overnight sensation, then you will fail. Those are short-term rewards that have nothing to do with growing your channel or brand. Instead, focus on creating consistent content that will engage your audience. The sweet spot to hit is that point of intersection between what your brand stands for and what your audience care's about.

Researching content topics

If you have an existing customer base or a following in another social media platform, you can create a questionnaire asking your existing fans what they'd love to learn from you. Social media users are very interested in sharing opinions and offering suggestions. If you don't have any followers, then take a look at your competitors and peers. Subscribe to their channel on YouTube; see what's working and where the gaps are. Read all the comments on their most engaged posts. These are all great places to get new title ideas and topics.

Once the research is done, it's time to get specific and decide on the types of keywords you'll focus on. If your channel is more educational and informative, you'll need more informational keywords. But if the content focuses on selling, you'll need more transactional keywords integrated into your video content, title, descriptions, and tags.

A content plan should be integrated with your calendar using software like Asana, Buffer, etc. You can also create your own using a spreadsheet. All you need to have in the columns is the publish date, title/description, status (in progress, completed, delayed), type of content, main keywords.

HOW TO STRUCTURE THE VIDEO CONTENT - A SIMPLE TEMPLATE

- Map out the first 15 seconds.
- Outline the key points

- Use the proven formula H.I.C.C (Hook Intro Content Call-to-action)

Hook

The hook is the thing that will grab attention and get people to watch the video. Include it at the beginning of your video within that 15-second window, so people don't click away.

The intro always helps the audience understand what you're going to cover, why they should listen to you or care, and also a bit about yourself as the host.

Content

This is the meat of your video. All the value goes into this section, and it should take up the most time because you will be giving people what you promised at the beginning of the video. For example, if you're a personal trainer, this part would be the actual workout to get my abs tight.

Call-to-action

Always have a call to action at the end of each video. Summarize what the video was about; especially if it was informational or educational, and then ask them to take action. Even if it was purely an entertainment video, you could still add a call to action by asking your audience to subscribe, like, share, or comment on the video.

Keep your video structure super simple by following the above structure until you get the hang of things. Then you can get a bit fancier.

COLLABORATING WITH OTHER CREATORS IN YOUR NICHE

As I said before, a strong content strategy always has a section for collaborations. The smart YouTubers understand the importance of leveraging this tactic. Still, you should know there are some advantages and disadvantages to using this method.

Pros:

- Collaborations are completely free, so it's a great way to tap into an existing audience without spending money.
- Gives you exposure to a new audience, which can be extremely beneficial for a young channel.
- Enables you to create more content.
- The quality of content improves because you always learn so much from these types of partnerships, especially if done with someone who has been around a lot longer than you.
- It's a powerful way to establish connections and build real relationships with people who share your

passion and a desire to serve an audience. Some of these collaborations might even turn into new lucrative opportunities.

Cons:

While I don't believe in disadvantages when it comes to creating collaboration because every experience has something to teach us (even those that don't work out), I can share a few things to become aware of.

- It will require a lot of upfront energy to get these relationships started. You are 100% responsible for getting their attention and making them interested in your offer.
- You will need to do many follow-ups when going after your list of potential collaborators.
- You might experience lots of rejection, and that's okay. Learn to handle these situations.

When doing collaborations, make sure you give and serve first. Don't be overly self-promotional. Most importantly, be authentic. The only way you're going to resonate with a new audience and have them interested in checking out your channel is if you are fully authentic, so don't try to "fake it" or "fit in." This will ensure you get the most out of that experience. I would also encourage you to go into it open-minded and focused on having fun. It doesn't matter how many people end up subscribing. Learn to take your mind off metrics and data and just be a passionate creator. That will make the influencer you're working with also appreciate the experience, as he or she will see you care more about serving the audience than getting subscribers, and that might lead to more collaborative opportunities.

HOW TO MAKE SURE YOU NEVER RUN OUT OF GREAT IDEAS

You'll hear many content creators talk about going through a "dry spell," and at some point, you might find yourself experiencing the same. So let's talk about how to handle these situations. The worst thing to do is force yourself to get on camera when you feel completely drained of value and inspiration.

I usually encourage my clients to take a day or a week away from the spotlight and reset. Sometimes the pressure becomes too much and causes our creative juices to stagnate. However, my advice only works if you already have enough content in the pipeline to allow you that "off-time." That's why I encourage you to batch your content creation and schedule them ahead of time. At a minimum, one week ahead. Some people prefer to schedule it a month in advance. Whichever frequency you choose, make sure you have enough ready-to-go content so that you're not rushing or banging your head against the wall because it's Monday morning, and you have nothing to post.

To help ensure you avoid running out of ideas, here some best practices.

- Once a week, sit with a Google doc and write down all the titles you would like to create content for.
- Always carry a pen and notepad or train your Siri to be on the alert for when ideas come to you as you're running errands, working out, driving, etc. Some of the best ideas come to us when we least expect.
- Download an app such as Evernote to help you capture screenshots, save and bookmark links that inspire you as you browse the Internet. You might come across an article or video that stirs up your creative juices, and there's nothing worse than trying to find that link (days later) on your long browser history.

A SIMPLE FORMULA TO GET OVER 100 VIDEO CONTENT IDEAS IN LESS THAN 20MIN.

Content Topic Generators

These are your easiest source of inspiration and content ideas. In less than twenty minutes, you could have content for a whole month. The list of content generators continues to grow, so be sure to keep checking for new ones. How it works is that these software apps use the most popular title formulas and fill in the blanks with your specific terms and keywords. Check out

1. Portent Content Idea Generator
2. ContentIdeator
3. Content Strategy Helper
4. Hubspot's Topic Generator

Buzzsumo

Head over to Buzzsumo and type in the keyword you want to talk about. What you'll see is a breakdown of all the most popular content based on social shares. It's a great way to know what people love, and when you find articles that are doing well, a video version of the same will likely perform great. With their free version, you're limited to a few searches, but it should be enough to get your juices flowing, and you can see what's done well in the recent weeks, months even a year ago.

Ubersuggest

This tool gives you a lot more than content ideas. It also shares keywords ideas and tells you which content is doing well based on search volume. It's a great way to see the top ranking sites and the content making them rank so high so you can leverage those titles as well.

Answer The Public

This tool helps you find all the questions people commonly ask about the keyword you type in. In just a few seconds, you can have an abundance of content ideas and similar keywords, all organized in an easy-to-read diagram that you could easily download. The tool offers keyword alternatives like comparisons and prepositions, as well as related phrases.

Quora

Quora is a trendy Q&A platform that has gained lots of traction in recent years. Head over to the forum and type in your keyword or topics that you want to be an authority on. Then look at all the questions asked in your niche and pick the ones people are most interested in. You can tell by the number of followers and the number of upvotes for the top responses.

Once you find a hot question, shoot a video with your best answer. Be as educational, informative, and helpful as you can in that video and try to be comprehensive with your reply so that when people click to watch the video, they can immediately see the value you bring and hopefully subscribe.

But you're not done yet.

Once you've published the video, head back to that original question in Quora. Answer it with a few words explaining your thoughts and letting people know you've shot a video with a more detailed answer. You can link the video here to drive traffic directly to your YouTube video. I recommend keeping a spreadsheet with the list of questions and a direct link, so it's easy to find them again once you've shot the video. It also helps you keep track of how performance because you can check once a month to see if people responded and voted you up. It's impossible with Quora to run out of ideas because you don't need to come up with any. Just find questions you can best answer on video.

Other forums where your readers hang out.

Aside from Quora and Answer the public, you can also check forums like Yahoo, Reddit, or specific industry forums where your audience most likely hangs out. You want to find questions, problems, complaints, or inquiries that people are bouncing back and forth in these forums.

Online Groups

These include Facebook groups, LinkedIn, Twitter Chats, Instagram Pods, etc. People get together to discuss interests, topics, or even complain about products or services that might belong to your competitors. Look for groups that don't allow lots of articles sharing to avoid spammy ones. The best groups or pods are those that have lots of questions and answers.

Industry Publications and Blog Comment Sections

Most people don't realize what a goldmine it can be to spend half an hour going through your favorite publication's comment section. Suppose you're a personal trainer or dietician, and you want to come up with amazing content. By browsing through big online blogs such as Bulletproof and other health publications, you're likely to come across a lot of great ideas from their readers. Sometimes readers will even ask questions or raise concerns over something confusing that wasn't covered. Those are the gaps your video content should fill. The demand is there, and your content can be the solution.

YouTubers You Follow

I already asked you in an earlier chapter to make a list of your top competitors. These are the people who are already crushing it in your niche. You need to be subscribed to their channels so you can learn and get inspired by them. Perhaps one of your competitors created content six months ago that's now a little dated, or maybe they only shared a brief overview of the topic. Still, you can go deeper and create something even better. That's your ticket to growth and value-adding.

Social media influencers you follow as well as those who follow you

With this hack, you want to research all your top social media profiles to see whom you follow or who follows you that shares great content. Take a look at what they engage with and see if there are any topics you can add to your content planner.

Webinars

Most people don't think about this when first getting started but given how popular webinars have become, it's a great place to get content ideas. Check out popular websites in your niche. Research the top influencers in your industry who usually do webinars and follow them to see topics they keep running webinars on. The most popular webinar titles would also be great for video content.

HARO (Help A Reporter Out)

Help a reporter out is a great place to see trending topics, and it can be an opportunity for your brand to be featured. When you share your expertise on the platform, a reporter can pick up your story and share it with the world giving you free publicity. But I am sharing this platform with you because by being on it, you get a glimpse of what people are looking for in terms of topics and stories.

Google

Google can show you trends (go to Google Trends) or related searches from the search bar as long as you have your keywords right. By clicking on the tabs labeled "Video," you can also see the top-ranking videos in your niche, which would also indicate what area to focus on. Google also added a section called "People also ask," - which is great to find more questions relating to your topic or keyword. All these are great spots for coming up with fresh and relevant content.

Self-help magazines

There's a reason why magazines like Men's health and Cosmo are so popular. These magazines tend to have extremely clickable titles. They know how to give people what they want. I have a friend who first opened my eyes to this little trick. Now I use it all the time. Whenever I am in a store, I always look for the magazine section to quickly browse through some of these popular magazines. You can do the same. Just take a quick snapshot of the titles that most resonate with you and add your own industry's words.

Amazon

Amazon is another excellent hack because it is an endless ocean of content. You can create a lot of "how-to" content or answer questions left in the comment section of books, apparel, or whatever else your niche focuses on. Since there's a book written on almost every topic under the sun, consider browsing authors in your industry and look for bestsellers. Then open to read the table of contents for title ideas. If you really want to hit a vein of gold, invest some time going through the comments people leave and compile them into more content ideas. Although this might take a little longer than twenty minutes, it'll be worth your time, and you will end up with ideas that last you a year.

DO YOU NEED A SCRIPT? YES OR NO?

While it would be easier to give a yes or no answer... the real answer is - it depends. As the content creator, you get to determine what's wrong or right for you. There is no one-size-fits-all in this scenario because some people swear by script writing and teleprompters. In contrast, others would rather die than script out their content. You can start with either and see which fits best. Still, suppose you're a complete newbie. In that case, I encourage you to practice scripting or, at the very least, create bullet points and prompters to assist you as you build confidence in front of the camera.

If you already know scriptwriting is not for you because you've tried it for a while and it didn't pan out, no matter what you did, then please skip over to the activity section of this chapter. But if you're still unsure and feel your confidence is still lacking, a script will be the best way to go. It can be as simple as having a bullet point on a sheet of paper dangling next to your camera, where you can easily read the main points. Or get a teleprompter and write out a killer video script. Remember, this isn't a movie screen-play. You're creating something for a social network, so the flow of it will have to be different. Here is a guideline to follow:

One. Get the basic elements right.

As we said before, you have a fifteen-second window on YouTube to grab the attention of your potential subscriber. If you miss that window, the user is likely to click away, and we don't want that. So prioritize the hook and flow of the content.

Create a basic model for your script that can be explained in 1min. Breakdown the main points so you can easily communicate your message without losing the viewer. People need to understand your concept quickly.

Make sure the audio is of excellent quality. Audio matters a lot! If you're going to add background music, make sure it doesn't overpower or disrupt your voice. Don't you hate it when you can't hear what the guy says in his cooking video because of the loud music? Don't do that to your audience.

Two. Have a strong point of view.

At the end of the day, your YouTube channel is supposed to show what your brand stands for. It's essential to have a clear point of view and confidently express it. People who struggle to share their opinions boldly rarely do well on this platform. Since we've gone through exercises in earlier chapters to determine your channel's identity and your target audience, be sure to authentically and confidently speak your opinion about the topic you cover.

Three. Pacing.

When writing out the script, be sure to pace yourself accordingly. Don't add too many filler words or create awkward silence in your content. Let it flow naturally as though you're sitting with a friend in Starbucks having coffee. And please don't be like those late-night infomercials guys who barely breathe between sentences. Don't rush yourself just to meet a certain deadline. Pace yourself, keep a steady tempo that is true to your personality.

Four. Include lots of emotional words and triggers.

Do you know why a video prank of a teenage daughter scaring the crap out of her mom performs better than a reporter talking about inflation? Simple. Emotional content will always get more views because people can relate to it more.

Five. Be clear, concise, and conversational.

Whether you create a detailed script or an outline, it's crucial to come across as conversational and concise. To help ensure you do this, I would encourage you to avoid writing very lengthy sentences when scriptwriting. Videos don't require too many words because onscreen visuals accompany them, so you don't have to worry about using big and complex sentences. If anything, stick to terminology and sentences that a 6th grader can easily follow.

Example template to follow:

The first fifteen seconds of your video make or break your chances of winning a potential subscriber, so make your introduction short, sweet, and attention-grabbing. Introduce yourself and the topic at the beginning of the script, and please remember to add a strong hook.

When it comes to scripting this part out, make sure the very first few lines contain the hook to keep people tuned in. Follow it up with a clear breakdown of what the audience will learn by the end of the video.

Example: *Are you freaking out because it's just a few weeks to your wedding day, and you still haven't shed those extra pounds for your big day? Fear not, because by the end of this video, you'll know exactly what to do to drop at least ten pounds in the next five days without ever hitting the gym! I'm Jenny, and for the past fifteen years, I've been helping couples look hot for their big day and that special honeymoon week. Let's get you lean and ready to enjoy your special day now!*

Main Content and Ask an engaging question

Once the intro is done, script out the main content. This is the meat of the video. I often like to include questions to keep the viewer's attention. Something simple that gives a yes or no answer should do it, and it's a great way to encourage people to comment. In this section, script out word for word what you're going to teach. Going back to the example I just shared, scripting out this section would require Jenny to write out exactly how the viewer will shed those ten pounds within five days. What are the steps? What secret hacks or ingredients should the viewer know about?

That is also where a story would come in handy. Suppose Jenny has experienced this process of transformation. In that case, she can talk about how she did it and managed to shed that weight before her special day. Perhaps it's one of her clients who has an incredible transformation story that could be interjected here with a few before and after snapshots. Storytelling will keep the viewer glued to the screen and give them a glimpse of how powerful this solution is.

When scripting your content, be conversational, don't use big words, and make it short and punchy. The more succinct you are, the easier it will be to edit the video, and the more engaging it will be for the viewer.

Summary and call to action

In this last part, as you bring the video to an end, I suggest you do a quick recap of all the good stuff they learned. That is especially important if you're teaching something. Otherwise, summarise the main idea and tie it back to your main objective if there's a specific action step like downloading something, signing up for an event or program, etc. When you have softer CTAs, you can actually sprinkle them throughout the video, such as *"before we jump into the main secrets I want to share, let me remind you to hit the subscribe button so you never miss another cool video like this one."* In the end, you can also say, *"If you liked this video, then give it a thumbs up and share it with a friend."*

ACTIVITY #6: CREATE AND SCHEDULE YOUR CONTENT

Now that you've learned how to plan your content and where to find great ideas, it's time for action. Create a list of the video titles you will be shooting over the next 90 days. Get your content calendar out and start brainstorming and researching using the various hacks you learned in this chapter. By the end of this exercise (before starting the next chapter), you should have ninety potential video titles mapped out on your content planner. Schedule a time to create, edit, and publish each content on a calendar. Don't worry if you just got a panic attack when I mentioned video editing. Yes, it can be a daunting process, but the next chapter two chapters are designed to ensure you have an easy and fun time. For now, let's put some ideas on our planner and prep ourselves for success.

Pro Tip:

If you want to stay focused and on-point with your content planning, fill out this simple statement, and let it direct your focus on content ideas. Keep this statement in mind, print it, and stick it where you can see it often, so you always stay relevant and interesting to your ideal audience.

Complete the following:

The video content I produce helps my brand accomplish ... [name goal]... and ...[name goal].... by providing ...[adjective]... and ...[adjective]... content that makes...[name emotion].... feel...me emotion]... or...[name benefit]... so that they can... [Name benefit]...

7

RECORDING YOUTUBE VIDEOS

*R*ecording your video should be as easy as switching on the camera and pressing the red button, right? Well, that's true, but there's a lot more that goes into recording. Lots of things have to be prepped beforehand. It's known as the pre-recording phase. Many items also have to take place once you're done recording (the post-production phase). Both the pre- and post-recording phases affect the video's overall result; so don't skip over this or the upcoming chapters. This chapter will focus on what you need to know and do to be camera-ready and produce amazing videos. So before you hit that record button, let's cover some best practices and also the type of equipment you'll need to make your YouTube channel successful.

THE ONLY EQUIPMENT YOU NEED TO GET STARTED

Video production can be costly; I won't lie. Some of these YouTubers have invested tens of thousands in having the recording studios, equipment and crew you see on their channels. I created this book with the simple intention of helping the beginner who may or may not have a budget available yet still wants to create something beautiful. If that's you, then this chapter will ease some of your concerns. Whether you can afford to spend a few thousand, hundreds, or zero dollars on equipment, I'm here to show you how to be camera ready. The essential gear you need include:

- A camera that can shoot in HD
- Good lighting
- Great Audio
- Video editing software
- Camera stabilizer or mounter

Whether you're broke or have some money to invest, these five things are fundamental to recording your video. I will break down some options for each of these for those serious about getting the right equipment, but even if you can't afford a dime yet, there are some simple workarounds.

Got zero money to spend? Read This.

If you have no money to invest in equipment, consider using your smartphone camera or the webcam from your laptop. Most of the smartphones come with incredible video quality. The minimum quality standard you need to go for with a camera should be 1080p. Make sure you also have a laptop with free editing software like iMovie (for Mac users).

Of course, you will need to mount the recording gear somewhere, so get creative. If you can't afford a stabilizer like a tripod, then stack some books or boxes on a desk near a window so that you can also get that natural lighting. When it comes to the audio, you can always use the phone or laptop's inbuilt audio system.

This isn't going to produce top-notch quality. However, you can still shoot pretty decent videos if you play around with a cool background and use editing and filters. For free graphics editing, you can use Canva, which is great for producing attention-grabbing thumbnails.

Got some money to invest? Read This.

HERE ARE SOME OF THE BASIC THINGS TO CONSIDER IF YOU CAN INVEST SOME MONEY INTO YOUR EQUIPMENT.

1. The Camera.

Get a camera that shoots in 4K. Since it's going to be the most critical piece of equipment, please invest to the best of your ability. If you have no limitations with your budget, then the sky is the limit. Your options are plenty. Quality camcorders or webcams (if you're using a laptop to shoot) are great for beginners. Still, if you can afford to spend a bit more, I suggest you go for a DSLR camera. How do you decide what to purchase? Think about your budget and the type of content you'll be creating.

Camcorders are designed to record videos. Hence they are the easiest to operate, light to carry around, and can handle almost any shooting scenario, whether your vlogging on the go or sitting in your basement studio. A good recommendation for this would be the Sony HDRCX405, which goes for about $198. What's great about it aside from the pocket-friendly price is that it is full HD with an image stabilization feature, which reduces shaking and blurring when shooting handheld. It can shoot 1080p videos at 60fps and is equipped with a Carl Zeiss zoom lens with 27x true optical zoom for lossless magnification and excellent overall video quality. It also allows you to record in MP4, which makes web uploads super fast and convenient.

For webcams, I recommend Logitech C920 HD Pro, which goes for about $89.99 and, of course, shoots full HD 1080p and 720p. If you're a gamer, this will be a perfect fit for you because the camcorder uses its own processor to encode videos instead of relying greatly on your computer power. That means it won't slow down your computer either, which is great.

The most favored and highly recommended cameras for YouTubers across all niches are DSLRs. That's what I use too, and I'm pretty happy with the quality. I love these cameras because of their adaptability in low light situations and the polished video recording quality they provide. But trust me, this is for someone willing to invest a bit more money. There are many great options, whether you prefer Sony or Canon, but I will share my two favorite options, both of which are Canon Cameras. The first is the Canon 70D, and the second is the Canon EOS Rebel T5i. Both are amazing, so do your research, and based on your budget and content needs, pick one.

2. The Microphone

There's no way around this. You need to invest in a lapel or an omnichannel microphone for excellent audio. Great audio doesn't just happen automatically. Even the best cameras need a little help when it comes to audio quality.

The microphone you choose doesn't need to be super expensive. You can get a Lav mic, which picks up less background noise and is pocket friendly. You can something decent starting from as little as $30 on Amazon. If you want to invest a little more, then here are some great options.

Get a USB microphone. These mics have become pretty popular with YouTubers because of their ease of use and sound quality. They are also pretty affordable. If you want to go, this route consider getting the Logitech Clear Chat H390, which goes for around $39.99. It's super easy to use and provides a clear, crisp sound. You could also go for Audio-Technica AT2020USB Plus, which goes for $149. What's great about this is that it allows self-monitoring through its built-in headphone jack with volume control. It offers mix control so you can blend your microphone with pre-recorded audio.

Go for shotgun microphones if you're serious about becoming a heavy hitter. You'll need to have deeper pockets for these types of microphones. They work great with a small professional camera and have shock mounts that help reduce the noise coming from mechanical vibrations around the mic. These types of microphones are known for capturing crisp sounds and vocals, even if you're recording outdoors. My recommendation if your pocket allows is to go for Rode Microphones VideoMic Pro R, which sells at about $299. It's a handy version that's perfect for your DSLR or camcorder. It comes with a super-cardioid polar pattern system and is powered by 9V batteries so that you can use it for up to 70 hours.

The last option I want to give you is a lavalier mic, aka lapel mic, and this is perhaps the easiest route to go. All you need to do is discretely clip it onto your clothes or belt. It comes in a set that includes a transmitter to which the lapel is connected and the receiver, allowing sound to be picked up even from great distances. If you're a speaker, you've seen these in conferences. My recommendation is RODELink Digital Wireless System, which goes for $399, so yeah, you'll need a big budget for this one. The benefits make it worthwhile because it works even from a hundred meters away and offers the ability to select the best signal to deliver audio that's as reliable as cable connections.

3.Lighting

Natural sunlight is, of course, one of the best lights you can have for your video. Still, you're not at a loss if nature isn't working in your favor as you begin this journey of YouTube stardom. As long as you can invest in some good lighting, even a small space in the basement can produce a high-quality video. Your setup's mood and brightness are influenced a lot by your lighting, so here are some options to make sure you come across looking like a professional.

The first recommendation is getting a softbox. It can emulate the natural soft lighting from a window. If you want to go with something subtle, this would be the ideal choice, and the best part is the Flashpoint SoftBox goes for only $49.95. It comes with a 70W fluorescent light unit and an AC plug that's easy to use. You can use this kit indoors with camcorders and digital cameras.

The second recommendation is a ring light. Ring lights are super popular with vloggers. When its ring shape emits light all around you, it eliminates shadows from every direction, making you look way more attractive in front of the camera. So next time you see those doll-like beauty vloggers - don't envy, just appreciate their creativity and lighting system! If you'd like a similar setup, experiment with Flashpoint 19 Kit. It uses 80W power that doesn't emit too much heat, so you could even have it closer to you, especially if you plan on doing close-up shots.

I would like to make one last recommendation if you need something lightweight that can be mounted on the camera. It's the iKan iLED-MA Micro Flood Light, which goes for about $29.99. It can emit a dimmable wide 120-degrees beam of bright 5000K+ Daylight with 21 1.2-watt LEDs. It comes with a MicroUSB cable for charging and a shoe mount that's fixed to a back holder so you can position it vertically or horizontally once it's on your camera.

4.The Tripod Or Stabilizer

Depending on how you shoot your videos, you can opt for a tripod or a gimbal stabilizer. They both accomplish the vital task of keeping your image steady, which increases production quality. Most beginners opt for a tripod, so I'd recommend you start there too. Most of them are under $100 on Amazon, and they work pretty well, especially if your camera isn't too heavy. If you need something sturdy and more durable, there are a few options out there that won't break the bank, including the iKan E-Image EG01A2, which is only $169. This tripod can handle most DSLRs and camcorders and holds up to 11lbs. Extension of this tripod is over 5 feet, making it easy to shoot from exciting vantage points. The best part is that it can collapse down to 33inches and weighs only 10lbs, making it ideal for travel.

For the gimbal stabilizer, I recommend the iKan FLY X3-Plus Gimbal Stabilizer, which goes for $69.99 is perfect for content creators who are continually shooting on the move. Let's face it, no matter how steady your hands are; handheld shooting will produce shaky and jarring videos. This particular gimbal is fantastic because it has a 3-axis stabilizer system with brushless motors that will smoothen out your camera movements. It also has a battery life that can last up to 5 hours! Talk about good value.

5.Video editing software

Post-production is just as important when aiming for high-quality video, so you must invest in some kind of editing software. If you have a Mac computer, of course, you've got the free iMovie that comes with it (Windows Movie Maker for PC users). Still, there are other products in the market you may want to consider.

There's a software that comes highly recommended by many of my peers, and it has a free version that a beginner can use to test out. It's called Hitfilm express. It has professional-grade VFX tools. They claim it's perfect for beginners, gamers, or any creative who doesn't have a budget. It might be worth checking out.

Adobe Premiere Elements 18 is an alternative many videographers promote. Of course, you need a budget for this and some skills, so give yourself time to learn how to use it best. If you'd like something a little easier to work with, I can also recommend Camtasia, which will be about $199. It's pretty easy to navigate and versatile. The learning curve is short, so if you're not too crazy about graphics and editing, that should sort you out. Need more software options? Keep reading this book as I cover more alternatives in an upcoming chapter.

For those who want to get really fancy, add the following equipment.

6.Digital Recorder

If this is the first time you hear the term "digital recorder," don't worry you're not alone. We've all had to learn what it is and why we need it. Usually, only the pros get this type of fancy equipment because they want to elevate that sound quality. At first, I was hesitant to invest in it, but after using it for a few years, I can't believe it took me so long to get it. A digital recorder is super useful because it enables you to transform any environment into a studio-like effect. If you like crisp, high-quality sound, this is going to be a worth-while investment. I especially recommend it if you'll be doing many interviews. A great one to start with is a Zoom H4N pro. It's handy, easy to carry around, and will last you a while.

7.Teleprompter

Another fancy piece of equipment you could get is a teleprompter to help you flow better with your script. It will ensure your message is on point and save you hours of filming and editing. Nowadays, there is a wide range of variety that can work with a camera or a smartphone. Amazon should have plenty of options to pick from, but you can always check out Caddie Buddy, which is pocket friendly and functional.

8.Get a studio backdrop

The last fancy equipment you can get is a studio background. If you're planning to have an indoor set up with minimum movement, consider getting a green screen, or whatever studio backdrop fits your budget. Some of these can be quite costly, ranging thousands of dollars, so do some research first. When I'm shooting, I just opt for a natural background in my home with a bookcase in the set showing some of the awards I've received over the years. Nothing fancy. For my personality and audience, it works. But suppose you want to go for something flashy. In that case, you can check out this inexpensive backdrop I found on Amazon for $58 called Slow Dolphin Fabric Video Studio Backdrop Kit.

One last recommendation I can make here is getting a large banner created with your branding. Depending on the size, it could be anything from $100-$500, but when designed well, it can be a great way to reinforce your brand and make you look super professional.

BEST PRACTICES FOR RECORDING YOUR VIDEOS

Make sure your video has a purpose.

Don't just shoot a video because you heard the topic is trendy or because you promised your audience to post daily/weekly. Each piece of content should be planned ahead of time. It should also serve a purpose. So ask yourself questions like, "what does this video want to accomplish? Is it views back to my website? New subscribers? More comments, likes, and shares?

I encourage you to get laser-focused on one specific target.

Make the video valuable and relevant.

Your video needs to add some kind of value to your audience and potential subscribers. Whether you're a comedian, gamer, vlogger, stylist, personal trainer, or coach, make sure the content you put out is relevant and useful. If you're an entertainer, make sure you entertain and leave the viewer feeling renewed and amused.

Do what it takes to have great audio.

You might not have the budget for investing in expensive equipment, but you can still produce good quality audio. If people can't hear you well, it doesn't matter how many filters and post-production software you use.

Always have a teaser at the beginning of the video.

Any type of video content you create should always have a tease at the beginning promising a specific result if someone watches the video all the way through.

Have a call-to-action at the end of each video.

Many YouTubers shy away from this because they are afraid of seeming pushy, but the only way people will turn into fans, customers, and subscribers is if you ask them to take action. Always ask them to do something if they received value at the end of the video and enjoyed watching your content. It can be a simple as subscribing or leaving a comment for you. You can ask the viewer to like, share, or DM as well. Or you take it a step further and can ask them to head over to your website to download something for free.

Lighting is so important if you want people to view more of your videos.

If people can't see you or hear you clearly, you won't retain their attention for very long. So equally as important as investing in good sound quality is having the right light. I shared lots of alternatives for lighting equipment earlier. Even if you can't invest in any, you can still create something that looks good if you stand in front of a large window. The more natural sunlight falls on your face as you record, the better the image quality will be.

#1 TIP FOR ALL BEGINNERS

The best advice I could give you is to shoot one video a day. It's the number one tip for all beginners who want to thrive on YouTube. If you ask any seasoned content creator, they will insist that you train yourself into the habit of creating at least one piece of content daily. Why? There are several reasons.

The first thing this will do is raise your confidence ability to shoot great videos. The more you practice using your equipment, experimenting with different angles, lighting, sound, and content topics, the easier it becomes, and the more natural you appear on camera. The second reason you want to shoot a video each day is to enable you to re-watch yourself and quickly pick up the mistakes you tend to make. Check your body language and posture. Notice how well you get into the flow and tempo of your script.

One last reason is that shooting videos daily ensures you have lots of content available, increasing your posting frequency. The more you can create a consistent publishing schedule whereby potential subscribers realize they can receive fresh, relevant content from you daily, twice, or three times a week, the more likely they are to subscribe and keep checking your channel for the latest stuff. It will build that connection and sense of community with your audience really fast. With all that said, I ask you to consider challenging yourself to attempt to create a video each day for the next 30 days. There are many "Video Challenges" and contests on social media groups today that you can join. Even without joining a group challenge, if you are serious about becoming a YouTube superstar, you can commit to yourself, block out time on your calendar over the next 30 days and begin.

Shooting techniques for beginners

Whether you're going to use a smartphone, camcorder, or a DLSR camera to shoot your videos, here are some tips that will give you that professional look even if you're a total amateur.

Tip #1: Always shoot landscape.

By landscape, I mean horizontally instead of vertically. That is especially important to remember when using your smartphone.

Tip #2: Use the overlay grid if you have it on your device and observe the Rule of thirds.

The Rule of thirds is something all pro videographers know. It's about placing your head slightly higher than the frame to give yourself visual breathing and walking space when facing the sides. Using a grid will guide you and help you position yourself properly so that you can maintain proper eye level with your audience. Otherwise, you will come across looking really awkward. The viewer will struggle to maintain eye contact as they watch you.

Tip# 3: Create stability for your camera.

You can invest in a tripod, or if doing a home video, you could get creative and stack books to help your camera remain still. The more still your image, the better the quality will be. Avoid shaky filming at all costs unless you want to come across as a complete amateur and give your viewers and nauseating feeling in the process. If you're going to be doing an outdoor recording with lots of movements, then investing in stabilizers and a good tripod is necessary.

A creative bonus tip that will make you look like a pro:

If you're shooting at home or in a home office, get a flat surface like a table and stack it with books. Place your laptop on top of the stack and if you're shooting from your smartphone, place the phone on the computer for extra support and stability. You'll be amazed by how good the shot will be.

Tip #4: Time your shots.

I've seen several pro videographers sharing these hacks, and ever since I started implementing them, my videos have improved significantly. You time your shots by ensuring there's no sudden movement or change of scenery for about 10 seconds between each shot. That means you need to record with that in mind. Every five to ten seconds, you can have a different scene but never go longer so that you can retain the viewer's attention. If you can keep this in mind when creating your outline or storyboard, your videos will come out looking way more professional.

Tip #5: Keep a simple background.

It might be tempting to be fancy and outlandish with your background, but simple tends to produce a better quality looking video. If you're shooting from home, remove as much clutter as possible. I also recommend shooting in front of a plain white background. Please avoid doors or windows where people could unexpectedly pop up and ruin the shot. If any elements show up in your camera, make sure they add to your story, not distract viewers from your content.

Tip#6: Be intentional with your lighting.

This has to be one of the biggest secrets for getting that professional look and feel. If you have a budget, then invest in the different types of lights you'll need to achieve your desired look. If you're on a budget and can only work with the natural sunlight and a few lamps, then get creative. Experiment with different angles and light setup so that you can make your equipment work for your particular space.

Tip #7: Experiment with different angles.

When shooting different scenes, I want you to create extra creative shots to produce interesting video content. It also ensures you have some backup or safety content in case you need to edit out some parts of the video. Get some shots above and below your main recording vantage point as much as possible. You don't need to have several cameras. Simply hit pause, move to a different angle, and hit record following the script or outline.

Tip #8: Keep the editing in mind during filming.

You need to know where you will make cuts, add filters, change scenes, and so on. If you have this in mind while shooting, it will make the filming and editing process faster.

SET AND FOLLOW A REALISTIC SCHEDULE

One thing you should know is most of the time, you're going to be completely off with your timings. I cannot emphasize the importance of setting the right expectations for yourself and creating a schedule you will stick to. Many YouTubers fail and give up because they didn't do a good job creating a schedule they could stick to. Most of them underestimated how long it would take to go through all the different shooting phases. Unfortunately, that led to stagnation, procrastination, and eventually defeat.

To help you avoid falling into that trap, we need to give you direction and a strict schedule that you must commit to. I can only offer guidance when it comes to creating your plan. You need to customize it to suit your needs. Depending on your lifestyle, whether you're currently working on other projects or a job, raising a family, etc., your schedule will match your particular case. If you're working full-time and need to start this after working hours, your shooting schedule and recording space and editing need to check that. Maybe you can shoot daily after work then edit and prepare them for publishing over the weekends. If you're flexible enough to shoot during the day and edit in the evenings, then make sure to build your schedule around that. Regardless of your choice, understand that you will need to set a definite time for scripting, recording, editing, and publishing the content.

Pre-production tips:

- Make sure you block out time for research, scripting, and even storyboarding if you're going in that direction.
- Plan out the different shots and scenes that you wish to have. I'd recommend making a shot list and, of course, ensure that you have the location or setup space needed for the shots as well as the necessary gear.

How long will a single shoot take?

That will vary from person to person. If you already have experience being on camera and you know how to use your equipment, you might get it done in a relatively short time. But more often than not, it takes much longer than any of us anticipate. So whatever estimate you give yourself permit at least 60 - 90 minutes longer.

To help minimize the time it takes, I encourage you to keep time limits on yourself. For example, set a five-minute timer to do all the technical set up. Also, give each scene a time limit and allow yourself the gift of reshooting a scene twice before moving on to the next big scene. That way, you won't have to recreate the whole thing.

Post-production tips:

So far, we've focused most of the content on shooting. We need to address post-production as well.

- Review your script, storyboard, or outline depending on what you're working on. This is important to ensure you filmed everything.
- Start the editing process. If you're doing the editing yourself, you need software like iMovie, Camtasia, or some other solution. You need to upload the different pieces of your video to the software and organize them in their proper order so you can decide what to keep and what to discard. If you got

enough coverage, it would be easier to pick and choose the perfect ones making this process faster.

If, however, you only shot once and there were many mistakes, give yourself time and patience. Such cases will require much refinement to get the video ready for publication.

What elements can you add to the video?

You can photos, b-rolls, interviews, titles, sound effects, transitions, intro and outro, music, and your logo.

Create thumbnails.

Use Canva or your preferred graphics creator software to create a compelling thumbnail for your video. Make sure it's attention-grabbing and that it helps the viewer know what the video will be about. We'll talk more about how to create epic thumbnails in an upcoming chapter.

Watch your video at least once before publishing.

Make sure you watch the video at least once with a friend or family member so you can get some feedback if possible. If you don't want that, watch it yourself to ensure the flow and quality are intact.

Once you feel it's ready, export it and upload it to YouTube. Depending on your level of experience, this entire post-production process could take an hour, a few hours, or several days. When just getting started, allow yourself a full day of post-production for each video if you want good quality. With lots of practice, that duration will significantly decrease.

If you decide to batch post-production, then shoot videos daily, edit them on the weekend and make sure you have enough videos ready to go for the upcoming week.

IMPLEMENTATION ACTIVITY #7: YOU JUST HAVE TO DO IT

It's time for you to take action and record your first videos. Your challenge in this section is to commit to a thirty-day video challenge. Keep yourself accountable and choose the setup and equipment most accessible to you. Every day you will shoot a ten-minute video that's valuable and relevant to the viewer.

You can choose to post-produce one by one or batch them up. But make sure the recording happens daily. By the end of thirty days you should have thirty videos of ten minutes each. Make sure they are of high quality technically, and that they deliver in terms of the content value.

8

EDITING VIDEOS

*V*ideo editing is an integral part of creating awesome YouTube videos. It can be as simple as removing unwanted footage, creating a flow, or as complex as adding effects, graphics music, and giving a video a particular angle. You can spend a few minutes to several days or weeks editing, depending on your editing goals. For beginners, I always suggest setting simple goals and striving for progress instead of perfection. If you want your videos to come out looking like a Marvel production in the first few months of editing, then be ready to invest a ton of time.

The best advice I can give is to understand the basics and to allow yourself to grow with your skills as you continue to shoot more videos. In this chapter, I will teach you the main elements, share with you the tools I recommend, and walk you through the process of adding music to your videos. Let's get started.

UNDERSTANDING THE BASIC ELEMENTS OF VIDEO EDITING

Before sharing the main elements, you need to consider when editing, let's clarify some of the jargon you'll hear a lot during this process.

Crop Factor

Crop factor is a number that represents the ratio of a sensor's imaging area to that of a full-frame sensor. It's usually 1.3-20.

Aspect Ratio

The relation between the width and height of your video is the Aspect ratio. The most common are 4:3 (This is the standard-definition video), 16:9(standard high definition video), and 1.85:1(used for most U.S theatrical showings since the 1960s). If there's one thing you'll need to remember, it's 16:9, as you'll be using that one the most.

Close Up

You'll hear this term a lot, and it means shots that frame the subject tightly. For example, if you were shooting in front of the camera, then a close-up would be filling the entire screen with your face.

B-roll

This is additional footage meant to either smooth out an incongruent scene or provide more details for the story being told. Suppose you're talking about cooking ingredients, and you want to shift into a new scene in which you start demonstrating. You could add a still image of the ingredients you'll be using to create a seamless transition from your talking head to you standing behind the kitchen counter ready to cook.

Jump Cut.

These types of cut should not be used unless you want to come across as an amateur. They are abrupt changes between sequential clips and often make the subject too jumpy from one scene to the next, which is very disruptive for the viewer.

J-Cut

Not to be confused with the other term; this is when you place the audio from the next shot before the actual video.

Resolution

Resolution is the actual number of horizontal and vertical pixels your video contains. The most common are SD 640x480, HD 1280x720 & HD 1920x1080

Shot List

This is a checklist of all the shots you want to include in the production. Shot lists help you avoid wasting time and money, and they ensure you plan ahead.

The Rule of Thirds

The Rule of Thirds is a helpful grid used when shooting to make your video production aesthetically pleasing. To do it properly, separate the screen into nine sections. The Rule of Thirds suggests that points of interest line up with the inter-sections on the grid.

- Tilts are vertical movements made with your camera that are fixed.
- Pans are fixed horizontal movements made with your camera. Think of them as the opposite of tilts.

The most important elements when it comes to video editing are:

Getting the pacing of the story right

Every video has a certain pace and tempo to it. Some scenes might need to be slowed down; others might need to speed up; and so on. When creating your video, be sure to create some breathing room for your viewers so they can digest the essential parts of your video. That might include changing the speed in certain sections but make sure the transition is smooth and gradual to avoid confusing the viewer.

Adding the right transitions and special effects

We already mentioned this earlier. Adding special effects during the editing process, such as titles, transitions, and text effects, is a great way to make your videos look professional, but only if you know what you're doing. If in doubt, don't add fancy effects. The more natural your video is (without too many abrupt transitions and confusing effects), the better it will look.

Choosing the right sound and music

That can include sound effects, audio background music, or anything else you think will make the video more impactful. Music usually adds a great atmosphere and increases that emotional connection, especially when done right. Make sure, however, that the music is non-intrusive and that it doesn't repel the viewer or obscure important audio cues.

Qualities of a Good Video

It's important to understand the technical and subjective things that cause both people and YouTube algorithm to perceive your video as good quality.

A good video clearly communicates a specific message.

If it's an educational, inspirational, motivational, informational, or entertaining video, the viewer will come out on the other side having received that particular benefit. Therefore a good video must add lots of value.

High quality

Producing a high-quality video is as simple as ensuring you follow all the instructions outlined in this book. They include no shaky imagery, proper lighting, and sound, avoiding noisy backgrounds, working on the script or outline, etc.

Clean and professional looking editing

This is another vital thing to remember when going through your post-production process. Keep things clean and simple. Only choose the best footage and eliminate what doesn't need to be there. Use elements like filters, music, sound effects, and transitions tastefully. Let everything on that video help you tell the story and pass on an easy-to-understand message.

Ideal length of content.

A good quality video isn't too long and boring or too short and unhelpful. You need to pick your ideal length and make sure it's as long as it needs to be to accomplish the video's purpose. We talked about giving each video a specific purpose to fulfill. Let that be the guiding star when it comes to determining how long your videos should be.

Attention-grabbing thumbnail and intro

Most people will never click on a video if the thumbnail isn't enticing. And do you know that about 20% of the people who do click on your video will exit after the first ten to fifteen seconds if you don't do a great job retaining their attention? What's even worse is that these people are more likely to give your video thumbs down within that first fifteen-second period. Therefore, you need to make sure you have a strong intro and graphics that draw people in.

Once someone sees your awesome thumbnail and clicks to view, you need to have a killer intro that immediately teases about why they should watch to the end. Set expectations right and make it feel personalized. That builds a connection that ultimately creates trust and that sense of "this guy/girl knows what they're doing."

Branded intro and outro footage

If possible, I suggest you add an intro and outro footage that aligns with your brand. This type of branded content imprints viewers, both new and existing, with an impression of who you are and why they should continue hanging out on your channel. It makes you memorable, especially if you do it right. Given how many videos are uploaded each minute of the hour, and most viewers watch hundreds of videos across different channels, adding this branded content to your video will make it pop. It will increase the viewer's chances of recalling your brand the next time they come across your content on YouTube or elsewhere on the Internet.

VIDEO EDITING TOOLS THAT EVERY YOUTUBER MUST KNOW

Now let's talk a bit more about editing tools that can help simplify the post production process.

Adobe Premier Elements

Adobe Premier has been an industry leader for a long time. It does cost a significant amount to get the software going for about $79.99. Now, there was a time when it was the ultimate; however, with recent advancements, many new players offer the same or even better at a fraction of their price.

It is still an excellent option for beginners and has many guided tutorials to make the learning curve swift. Its simple interface and guided edits will get you going in no time.

Adobe Premier Pro

As the name suggests, this software goes pro, and it offers you some of the best functionality you can find in the market today. One of its best features is the Lumetri Color tool, which features color adjustment and manipulation that's pretty close to what you'd get on Photoshop. It also has a multi-cam feature, which allows you to work with an unlimited number of camera angles. The interface is easy to use even for a beginner and comes with a monthly fee of under $20.

Apple iMovie for Mac users.

Suppose you are a Mac user and don't wish to invest in third-party software. In that case, you can create cool looking videos with Apple's free editing software, which offers various transitions, sound effects, etc. You can easily do a montage, standard cut, J-cut, wipes, and almost every other editing effect you can think of. It's free and easy to use once you get the hang of it.

Apple Final Cut Pro X

If you love iMovie and feel ready to go all the way, then this software might be the one for you. This software comes with all the bells and whistles and can even superimpose 3D titles over your videos. It comes with a hefty price tag and isn't necessarily the most straightforward interface, but if you want to be a serious contender and produce incredible professional videos, then you can make the transition from iMovie to Final Cut Pro for a one-time payment of $299.99

Filmora from Wondershare

Filmora is Wondershare's standard, high quality, and easy to use video editing software. You can upgrade to unlock more sophisticated features. Still, I suggest starting with this one because the design is intuitive. It has filters, overlays, motion elements, transitions, and much more - so, basically, every-thing you need as a beginner. I love Filmora because all it takes is an easy drag and drop. You can choose themes, select free royalty music, and end up with a fun, polished video thanks to their easy mode feature. And compared to some of the prices I just shared, this one isn't too bad because it starts at $59.99 for a lifetime license or $39.99 for a year.

Pinnacle Studio 21

Pinnacle Studio 21 is another great and easy to use software with a drag-and-drop feature. It's intuitive, has a short learning curve, and has effects like 360-degree and stop-motion, making it stand out. It has top of the line rendering speed and goes for a one-time payment of $129.95

Lumen5

While Lumen5 is more of an editing tool than software, I am still adding it here because of its increased popularity. It's great for creating fun, shareable videos, and it can even turn your blog content into video. So if you have an existing blog, this is a great option for you. You can create as many videos as you want with their free version for 480p videos. If you want 1080p HD, then you'll need to invest $50 per month.

Adding Music to Your Videos

Background music can elevate your video and help build a stronger connection with your audience, but you can't just throw in any song. You need to become aware of copyright restrictions and opt for royalty-free music. You should also choose music that supports the unfolding story or message of the video. I bet you're wondering where to find great music, right?

YouTube does offer some music options, and some software come in-built with sound effects and free royalty music, but I recommend you do some research online. Go to sites like epidemic sound or royalty-free music to find lots of stock music that you can use.

Adding music to a video using Mac: Once in the iMovie interface, you should see the Audio tab under the main menu bar within your new project. A drop-down menu will appear, giving you options to go into iTunes, Sound Effects, or GarageBand. In most cases, you just need to select iTunes and you'll see a list of all your files. Then all you have to do is drag it down to the project timeline. If you need to trim the song, just use the handles at the beginning and end.

Adding music to a video using Windows: Double-click a video file to open it and you'll see it opens in Movies & TV. Instead of that option, right-click the file and select Open With > Photos. You'll see a toolbar; click Edit & Create and then select Create a video with text. You'll then see Photos's editor screen, and in the top toolbar, there should be a Music button. Click that and select your Music. After choosing the file, drag your selected clip down to the story-board at the bottom of the screen. And when you play, you should hear music in the background.

Adding music online: Visit addaudiotovideo.com and you'll have the option of adding music to your video without downloading any software. It's fast and simple. Once on the site, click Browse under "Select video file" to choose the video. Next, you want to choose the audio file as well by clicking Browse. Once you've chosen both audio and video, click on Upload and give it a few minutes. Once it's ready, you'll see a message that says "Completed" and a download link.

YouTube Music: If you'd like to use YouTube's Audio library once you upload the video by clicking on the Editor and looking for the audio row. You'll see a list of tracks that you can listen to, and once you find what you like, just add it to your video. If you'd like to adjust which part of the audio is played during your clip, click the Position Audio button, then click and drag the song's leading and trailing edges to adjust their position.

ACTIVITY #8: START HONING YOUR SKILL

The videos you've started creating from the last chapter now get to experience your artistic. Your assignment is to begin implementing all the editing techniques, hacks, and guidance you've received in this chapter.

Remember, this is a skill that takes time and practice. As with all things, it will get easier. I suggest you allocate time specifically for editing your videos, whether you do one at a time or batch a few of them together. You can choose to opt for free software or invest in one of the many examples I've shared throughout this book.

Your assignment now is to open up your editing software, upload your first YouTube video, and start editing. See if you can add a few transitions, a title, and background music to create an attractive flow with your video. Don't get too fancy. Keep it simple. Once it's ready, give it to a trusted friend or family member to watch for some helpful feedback.

IV

MANAGING YOUR YOUTUBE
CHANNEL

9

BEST PRACTICES ON MANAGING YOUR YOUTUBE CHANNEL

One thing about YouTube that you need to keep in mind is that it's both a search engine and a social networking platform. So while it's important to implement everything you've learned so far, I also want you to be deliberate with certain aspects of search engine optimization, as that will enable your videos to perform well long-term.

Brian Dean of Backlinko is a specialist in search engine optimization, and you can learn a lot by subscribing to his YouTube channel. But let's touch on the key things I've learned from the best SEO guys in the marketplace.

CREATING VIDEO TITLES, DESCRIPTIONS, AND TAGS

Assuming you have a comprehensive list of the keywords you wish to rank for in any particular video, the title, description, and tags are the areas in which you need to sprinkle those pre-determined keywords strategically.

YouTube Video Title has a limit of 100 characters, so you need to use this space to build curiosity, create an emotional response for the viewer, and still add your keyword. Aim to place the main keyword at the start of the title as much as possible or at least within the first 70 characters so that it's viewable in the search results.

YouTube Video Description has a limit of 5,000 characters, so you've got plenty of space here to clearly communicate your message and add relevant keywords. The first three lines are the only visible part of the description, so I recommend having your primary keyword here. You also need to describe and sell the viewer into watching the video here. Remember to also include the relevant URL that you'd like people to visit after watching your video.

Throughout the description area, I'd say aim to sprinkle the primary keyword about three times and perhaps other secondary ones to support your SEO.

YouTube Video Tags can be up to 30 characters in length, and you can add up to 500 characters in the tag section. Add the primary keyword, any words that describe the video's content, brand-related or channel-specific tags, and any LSI (Latent Semantic Indexing) keywords you might have.

YOUTUBE THUMBNAILS

To get potential subscribers to click on your videos, you need to create thumbnails that stand out and attract the viewer. Thumbnails are also the first thing searchers will come across on Google and YouTube search results. The first thing you need to know is the ideal size. Google recommends 1280 by 720 Pixels with a minimum width of 640 Pixels and an aspect ratio of 16:9. It should also be formatted as a JPG, PNG, or GIF for the best results. Make sure the file size doesn't exceed 2MB for easy upload.

When creating your thumbnails, some things to keep in mind are to use attention-grabbing texts, fonts, color, and images but don't overdo it. Ensure the thumbnail is relevant to the content people will find once they click and that it's congruent with your brand identity.

If you're working with a graphics designer, then they'll take care of these technical aspects, but if you're going solo, then I suggest using Canva. They are a free graphics design software that requires little to no experience and even have pre-made templates. You can also purchase their royalty-free images for $1, and they offer a pro version that unlocks even more features. Another tool that can help you create awesome thumbnails is Spark by Adobe. Check out both these online tools to find the one that suits your objective.

UPLOADING VIDEOS

Uploading videos to YouTube is as easy as signing in to YouTube Studio, and clicking Create > Upload Video. Once you've selected the video you've finished editing and processing, YouTube will take over and do its thing until the video is completely ready for publishing. The video file format recommended is: .MOV, .MPEG4, .MP4, .AVI, .WMV, .MPEGPS, .FLV, 3GPP, WebM, DNxHR, ProRes, CineForm, or HEVC (h265)

If you want to upload a video that is longer than 15 minutes, you will need to go through a quick verification process where they will send you a security code through your cell-phone. Once your channel is verified, you can upload up to 12hours or 128GB.

You can upload up to 15 videos at a time using your computer. And don't worry if you accidentally close the upload page. The video is usually saved in drafts until you finish choosing the settings.

If you want to upload high dynamic range (HDR) videos, you can also do it directly to the platform. Viewers can watch HDR videos if they have compatible devices or can stream HDR videos using Chromecast Ultra to an HDR TV. If the viewers don't have a compatible device, they will see the video as a standard dynamic range (SDR) video. Although HDR videos can't be edited with YouTube Web editor once the video is uploaded, YouTube will automatically convert HDR video to SDR.

Once the video renders and completes processing, you can add basic info, including a SEO-friendly title, description, tags, and upload your thumbnail. You can also choose some more advanced settings and how you want to monetize if you're eligible. We'll be talking more about monetization options in the last section. If you're happy with the settings and preview of your video, it's time to share it with the world.

CREATING A TRAILER VIDEO

The trailer or welcome video can be one of the most fun activities you engage in. It doesn't need to be an expensive production. But it will require lots of creativity and time investment. I've seen some pretty epic trailers (check out the Slow Mo Guys Channel Trailer to see what I mean). You can start from scratch, or you can get a template from online platforms like Biteable to simplify the process.

The actual process of a welcome video is super easy. Like any other video content, you will have to create, edit, upload, and hit publish on your channel. The only difference is that with a trailer video, you want to head over to the "Customize Channel" section and upload the video from there. Once uploaded, you can add SEO-friendly data like tags, description, and so on. The last thing you will need to do is set the video as the YouTube channel trailer by clicking "For new Visitors." That way, anyone who lands on your channel for the first time will always see that video first.

Some best practices for the trailer video:

Keep the video brief and concise (under 30seconds is ideal). Think of it like those epic movie trailers and make sure you share all the necessary information about your channel. Your viewers should feel like they understand what you're all about and how they'll benefit by subscribing, but it should still leave them hungry to learn more.

The best trailers have a great story, implement their brand identity through the music, fonts, colors, etc. and always incorporate a call to action.

CATEGORIZING YOUR VIDEOS INTO PLAYLISTS

YouTube playlists are a collection of similar or related videos on a particular subject. You can create a playlist using your own videos or curate other people's videos to get people to binge-watch and stay on your channel. It will help with the discoverability of your channel and increase watch time, which, as we know, will help rank your videos higher on search.

To create a playlist, go to Video Manager > Playlist, then select New Playlist. Give your playlist a name and click Create. You can also create playlists as you navigate YouTube. This is especially important if you're curating videos. When you find a video you'd like to curate, simply click the plus icon to either add to an existing playlist or create a new one. You can make your playlist public, unlisted, or private depending on your preferences. It's also possible to optimize your playlist for search by editing the playlist title and description with a specific keyword and a compelling explanation telling people why they should watch.

Pro Tip:

If you want your playlists to stand out, consider adding an intro welcoming the viewer and offering some tips or letting the audience know what they can expect by going through each video on the playlist. This can work exceptionally well if you're creating an educational video series.

CREATING YOUTUBE STORIES

If you're a fan of watching YouTube from your smartphone, then you already know about YouTube Stories. Previously known as YouTube Reels, these are pretty similar to Instagram or Snapchat Stories. They can only be viewed on the mobile App. Viewers access them either from the channels or Watch pages of their subscriptions.

The purpose of YouTube stories is to increase that bond and connection with your community. It needs to be done in a very informal and casual way. You need to make sure it's a regular activity so people can get used to interacting with you directly.

You can add an image or video to a YouTube Story. To add a photo, tap the capture button like you would when taking a regular photo. If you want to record a video, press and hold the capture button until you're done recording. Stories videos can only be 15 seconds in length, so make sure it's short and sweet. There are plenty of editing tools available to add elements that will help make your content more appealing. You can also edit aspects of your recording and even delete an existing video or image from your story. Tap the story and tap the play segments to navigate to the video or image. Look for the three-dot menu and tap Delete.

APPLYING SEO

Now let's talk about ranking factors as well as how to apply SEO to your videos. Throughout this book, we've discussed the importance of using keywords strategically. As I shared earlier, there are ranking factors that Google says are important. Things like relevancy, interest, and so on. I think you will agree with me; there has to be more that we can do to stand out.

Given that over five hundred hours of video are uploaded each minute, we need a lot more tools and techniques to make sure our videos get promoted by the algorithm. Here are a handful to add to your toolbox. You already know the basics, i.e., Keywords, title optimization, description, tags, and producing high-quality video so let's talk about new ones.

Watch Time

Watch time is a huge ranking factor for YouTube. It's essentially the length of time a viewer spends on your video before clicking away. The longer a session, the more the algorithm will favor your content.

User Experience and Engagement Level

That includes how much people comment, like, dislike, share, and even subscribe after watching your content. Video with higher engagement will be ranked higher.

View Count

Getting many views on your video matters. Simply put - more views equals higher ranking, especially if you've done your keyword optimization right.

Closed Captions & Subtitles

Adding closed captions to your videos benefits you in multiple ways. The main two are: 1) you get crawled by search engines faster, which can give you a significant SEO boost; 2) you open up your content to a broader audience. People who are not natives in your spoken language can easily understand you, increasing the chances of more engagement and subscription to your channel.

MASTERING THE USE OF YOUTUBE ANALYTICS

The only way your channel will grow successfully is by combining front-end creative efforts with backend tracking and monitoring. YouTube comes with an in-built analytics system to enable you to track the right metrics and build your dream business. To get started, you will need to sign in to your creator studio and find your way to the main menu's analytics Tab. By default, you'll see the last 28days, but you can customize it to suit your needs.

If you enjoy data crunching, YouTube gives you the ability to export datasets as Excel or CSV. For most of us, however, I suggest letting the system do the manual work. All we need to monitor and track, especially at the beginning, are:

- Watch time reports
- Interaction reports
- Revenue reports

With watch time, you want to answer questions such as, how long are people watching my videos, and how many views do I have in the chosen timeframe? Is it the same as last month? Who is watching my videos? Where are my viewers located? What are some sources of my traffic? What percentage of my views comes from mobile, desktop, or elsewhere?

Interaction reports will show you things like subscribers, likes, dislikes, comments, and sharing. You can see how many new people subscribed and how many unsubscribed. You can see how your audience feels about your content and whether they are resonating with your message or not.

Monitoring comments is also important because it gives you a sense of how active and engaged people are. Remember to be responsive but don't get sucked into the world of troll hunting or toxic people.

When it comes to revenue reports, this is all about the monetization of your money. It's what you've been waiting to hear about because your money is going to be recorded here. In the next section, we do talk more about monetization and how to do it right. For now, recognize that this is where you will come to monitor your revenue within a given time period, including your own paid ads on YouTube, Ads other companies are paying to display on your videos, and other income streams like YouTube Super Chat. The main thing to track here is the estimated income from all Google-sold ads and the projected income from AdSense and DoubleClick ads.

PROMOTING YOUR CHANNEL ON OTHER SOCIAL PLATFORMS

It's essential to think outside the box when it comes to growing your channel. You need to be discovered, and your channel needs to get out of obscurity. Everything outlined in this book will enable you to set the right foundation for that, but you can't stop there. Social platforms like Facebook, Instagram, Tik Tok, and LinkedIn have so much traffic.

With a little creativity, you can help get more views on your video. How? By driving that traffic toward your YouTube channel. You don't need to get in front of YouTuber users only. You can also leverage both organic and paid strategies to promote your channel on other social platforms.

For example, you can write articles on high traffic sites like LinkedIn or Medium and embed a video or link back to your YouTube for free. But of course, with a little paid ads budget, you could take it a step further. Do this by creating an epic video ad for Facebook or Instagram that drives traffic back to your YouTube channel for the full experience. Once you look at your YouTube analytics and determine the location and audience type that best engages with your channel, invest a little money and run a highly targeted ad on Facebook to bring in more of the same people. To learn more and expand your traffic source strategies, please refer to the resource section.

CONTINUOUSLY LEARNING FROM OTHERS

As you can tell, this book is only the beginning. Something easy to follow to help you gain some momentum. The journey is long, and there's much to learn, so make sure you continue educating yourself as the platform evolves and new hacks come about. One way to stay up to date and learn the best and latest hacks is by following and initiating friendships with fellow YouTube creators. You can join meetups either locally or virtually. You can also attend events like VidCon or Social Media Marketing World. In the resource section, I have included links to learn more about these opportunities.

ACTIVITY #9: START TINKERING AROUND

This chapter shared lots of technical knowledge that will only work if you choose to apply them to your daily activities. If you haven't worked on any previous exercises, now is the time to do that. Once you have that video ready to share with the world, make sure to also include the things you've learned in this chapter, including:

- Creating your thumbnail.
- Uploading your video into YouTube.
- Customizing and optimizing the video titles, descriptions, tags, and any other effects you wish to have, such as music, captions, and subtitles.
- Follow a YouTube creator that you would like to learn more from as you grow your channel.

10

GROWING YOUR COMMUNITY

*Y*ouTube is all about community engagement. If you're not willing to put in the time and effort to build a connection with your tribe, you won't do very well on this platform. Having read this far, I'm confident you want to grow a channel that serves your tribe and makes you money. To hit both targets, we need to understand some strategies that will enable us to draw in more eyeballs.

SOURCES OF TRAFFIC

Do you know all the different ways your video can be discovered on YouTube? I've mentioned several already throughout this book, but it's worth listing them all here.

- YouTube search
- YouTube advertising
- External websites
- Browse features
- Suggested videos
- A particular playlist or channel page.

You need to figure this out as your channel grows so you can refine your SEO efforts and invest in the right strategies.

USING THE AUDIENCE TAB

Did you know that YouTube Analytics offers an inside glance into your audience's behavior, location, and preferences? This tab shows you where most of your viewers are located, the language they speak, what they love watching most, and their age group. To see this, you need to be signed in to your YouTube Studio. From the left menu, select Analytics > Audience. That will open up information on gender, age, when your viewers are on YouTube, and other videos your audience watched. Use this data to inform your content strategy.

ENGAGING YOUR AUDIENCE

As a YouTuber creator, your job isn't done until you interact and engage with your audience. A few things that work really well for engaging my audience include initiating engagement myself. That means I don't just post and wait for something to happen. Instead, I go and find content that's meaningful to me, and I like, comment and share that content. I also reply to every comment, and I intend to do that until they become too much for me to handle. On weekends, I've set aside twenty minutes to go to the channels of people who have liked or engaged with my content. I do the same on their channel, which creates amazing rewards later on.

Consider asking questions that benefit your community and encourage them to interact. The bottom line is you need to give more than you ask of your community. If you observe highly engaged channels from YouTubers like Gary Vaynerchuck or Neil Patel, you'll see they always give, give, and give before making any ask.

Pro Tip:

If you're really serious about showing your community that you care, take a screenshot of a comment left on your video or a video title that someone you want to promote shared and create a video out of that featuring their content. It will cause the person to respond immediately and even share your video.

YOUTUBE COMMUNITY TAB

This is a feature YouTube designed to promote community interaction. It's meant to help you interact even more with your people beyond creating and publishing videos. You will have the ability to post polls, text-based posts, and images.

This feature is meant to give your channel a different edge and to get even more personal. You can also promote older videos or products and merchandise. Make sure, however, you balance the promotion and the value-adding interactions. I find it to be an incredible way to get people excited about something you're doing. It could be the launch of a new product, an announcement of a free webinar, or training. I have used the Poll feature to get ideas of what to include in my online course to make it more valuable. My friend Jeremy uses it to give behind-the-scene sneak peek of his latest documentary shoots, which gets people really excited. The most important thing is to come from a place of adding value. Give people a reason to interact and follow your updates using the Community Tab feature.

MAXIMIZE THE USE OF LIVE STREAMING

What is Live Streaming? It's being able to record and broadcast in real-time simultaneously. YouTube has become pretty famous for live streams, and it is the perfect way to retain or draw in a new audience. You will need to educate yourself on the best equipment for live streaming, but YouTube enables you to go live from your smartphone or tablet, a camera, or a computer. Once you get the equipment sorted, it takes one click of a button.

Before attempting to go live, make sure your channel is verified (www.youtube.com/verify). If doing it from a computer, you need to sign in to your dashboard and click Create > Go Live. From your mobile, you will need to open the YouTube app and click the camcorder icon on the top right, then tap Go Live. If it's the first time to live stream, you will need to wait for 24hrs to activate your account. Also, note that you will need to hit your first milestone of 1,000 subscribers before live streaming from your mobile.

When it comes to the recording, you can either do it through a webcam, mobile cam, or encoder streaming. The easiest option is the camera on your laptop, but if you want a more professional look and have the competency, you can always get an encoder because the quality will be better.

To ensure you produce the best live streams, have your thumbnail image, an SEO friendly title, and description ready to go. If you're ready to record from your desktop, all you need to do is click the camcorder icon once you're in your dashboard >Go Live > Webcam. Add a title and privacy settings, then click More Options to add the description, enable/disable live chat, promote something, and so much more. Click Next. YouTube will automatically take a webcam thumbnail photo but don't worry because you can upload the thumbnail we just created later on. Select Go Live, and that's it! Once you're done, you can select End Stream.

A CHECKLIST FOR OPTIMIZATION

Here's the beauty of live streaming - it's live. There are no do-overs or edits. So before you begin to broadcast, take the following steps.

- Check the audio to make sure the sound is optimal and that people can hear you.
- Adjust your lighting to ensure the audience can see you clearly.
- Keep the devices plugged into a power source. You wouldn't want to run out of power halfway into your rant!

- Test your connection speed to avoid low-quality streaming. You can run a speed test with speedtest.net. What we are aiming for is about 10MB of data per minute.
- Turn off interruptions and make sure nothing inappropriate or confidential is in the backdrop.
- Have a bottle or glass of water next to you. I also recommend tissues or anything else you might need in case you get a scratchy throat, cough, or sneeze.

When it comes to live streaming, timing is everything. There's no perfect time per se, but based on your YouTube analytics, you can make an educated guess based on your audience interactions and behavior. If most of your audience is global, you want to pick a time that works in multiple time zones.

Pro Tip:

As your audience grows, you can consider running polls for people to vote the best time for the live streaming and once you have a winner, schedule it in advance. Give people time to add it to their agenda and set reminders.

ACTIVITY #10: WHAT MOVES YOU?

Before we hit the last section of this book, it's time to start engaging with your potential audience. You may not have any subscribers yet (aside from friends and family), but you can still create that momentum for engagement. Whether your published videos have received many comments, shares, and likes or not, you can find channels worth interacting with. Leave a comment, like, and share it. Repost it using your Community Tab, as you learned in this chapter. Demonstrate that you are here to build an active community. It all begins with you.

V

MONETIZE YOUR YOUTUBE CHANNEL

11

YOUTUBE MONETIZATION
MADE EASY

or many readers, these last two chapters contain the answers to critical questions that led them to purchase the book. If you have been wondering how to make money on YouTube or what kind of money you could make, this is where you'll get your answers. How much money do YouTubers make? Some make zero, while others make millions in annual revenue. The range is pretty huge because it depends on how well the channel performs.

HOW MUCH CAN ONE EARN ON YOUTUBE?

The best way to approach this question is to start from what we know YouTube pays out. We know that Google pays 68% of their AdSense revenue. Some quick mathematics will show you that if an advertiser pays $100, Google will pay

$68 to the publisher. The rates that an advertiser pays will vary between $0.10 to $0.30 per view, but let's go with an average of $0.18 to make calculations easier. So on average, your channel can receive $18 for every 1,000 ad views ($3-$5 per 1000 video views).

While these simple numbers can help you estimate what you can expect, realize the first dollar will be the hardest one to earn. Building up to that momentum will require a tremendous amount of effort, but the subscribers you have, the more people will click on your ads. The more that happens, the more money you will make from

Google AdSense and other opportunities. So the right answer is - you can earn as much money as you want. It all depends on your effort and strategy.

If you're in a niche that quickly gathers crowds like celebrity gossip or gaming, then you'll likely start to earn money sooner but still don't expect it to be within the first couple of videos. In the first phase of your YouTube growth, you want to focus on building a reputation instead of income. Then as you get real traffic and engagement, you'll start to see the revenue growth from a few dollars each other to hundreds and, ultimately, thousands of dollars each month.

THE SIMPLEST WAY TO EARN MONEY FROM YOUTUBE

The simplest way to earn money from YouTube is to join the YouTube Partner Program (YPP).

Before you can become part of this program and start earning money, you will need an audience. Your content has to be epic to attract an audience that engages with your content and subscribes to your channel. Everything discussed in this book is designed to help you attract, build, and ultimately monetize your audience. Once you have some momentum and you see constant growth, I recommend applying for the YouTube Partner Program.

To qualify for YPP, you need to be in good standing with YouTube. Your content should be considered high quality. You also need 4,000 public watch hours within the last 12-month period. Lastly, you will need to hit that target of 1000 subscribers. These basic requirements are vital before your qualification can be accepted. Once you cross this threshold, you'll be taken through a process of creating an AdSense account and a few other simple logistics. YouTube team will review and approve you for monetization. Besides streaming ads, you will also have the ability to earn through channel membership and Super Chat as long as you meet their criteria.

ACTIVITY #11: BECOME A YOUTUBE PARTNER

This particular activity will require time, so I recommend adding it to your planner or setting a timer so you can come back at the designated time to complete it. Once the channel continues to grow in the coming months, and you cross that threshold of 4,000 watch hours within 12 months and 1000 subscribers, please submit your application for the YPP monetization opportunity.

12

CREATIVE WAYS TO MAKE MONEY ON YOUTUBE

*N*ow that you've established a great YouTube channel that is steadily growing, it's time to focus on making money. If you want to start seeing income from all your hard work, combining several revenue-generating strategies might be the right approach.

Instead of depending on earning directly from YouTube (YPP), which requires a specific number of subscribers and strict watch time regulations, you can leverage other money-making options such as affiliate marketing, sponsorships, etc. Let's go over the main ones now.

BECOME AN AFFILIATE

Affiliate marketing is one of the easiest and most lucrative ways to earn an income on your channel. The best part is that you don't even need a huge audience. In recent years, brands have been seeking micro-influencers and social media channels with decent size following and lots of engagement to help promote their products.

Franck is a great example of this. He was approached by a software company about a month ago and gave him a very enticing offer. Franck was provided the free software to use for six months for free and would earn a percentage for every person who signed up and purchased through the affiliate link they gave him. The best part is that Franck has 2400 subscribers! It's only been a few weeks, and he's reported that a portion of his audience has signed up for the free trial, and some have paid. Income is already coming in, and soon, he will be making a projected $7k in passive income.

Affiliate marketing is simple. You have a product you believe in and a link where you can send people. Whenever people buy, you get a small commission. If it's a well-priced product, a few sales each month can earn you anything from a couple of hundred to several thousand. I know YouTubers who also run affiliate products from Amazon and ClickBank. These are massive affiliate platforms that anyone can join. But I suggest doing this once you have an active audience.

BECOME AN INFLUENCER

Influencer marketing is all the rage. Stay-at-home moms, artists, beauty specialists, and high school students have all turned their love for selfies into income-earning opportunities. What is an influencer, and can you become one on YouTube? An influencer is a person who can affect the purchasing decisions of others because he or she is perceived as an authority in that given niche. Influencers have strong relationships with their audience - that's what makes them powerful. An influencer is not a celebrity and doesn't need to be a Kardashian with millions of followers. The size of his or her following depends on her niche or topic. Brands are always keen to work with influencers of all sizes.

If you can build a reputation as someone knowledgeable and an expert in your topic through your YouTube content, you can become an influencer. As a result, you can get paid partnerships, collaborations, and sponsorships with the brands that align with your channel. There are various types of influencers, including mega-influencers (think Kardashians). These are often celebrities like movie stars, musicians, athletes, etc. To join this rank, you will need to have at least 1 million followers. Macro-influencers are a step down from the mega influencers. These are usually up and coming B-grade celebrities or super successful self-made online experts. To join this rank, you'll need to have at least 40,000 followers on YouTube. Micro-influencers are the first significant milestone I would set for you. This category of influencers are ordinary people who have gained respect and recognition for their knowledge.

You can create a relationship with your subscribers, and over time, they will see you as someone worth following and turning to for advice. In this category, it's not so much about the number of followers. It's absolutely about the relationship and engagement level. So a micro-influencer can have between 1000 - 40,000 followers on YouTube. Franck is an excellent example of how a brand perceived him as a micro-influencer and offered him the chance to collaborate through affiliate marketing. The same thing can happen to you. The most important thing to remember as an influencer is that you need to maintain your integrity and only promote brands you genuinely believe in.

Once you are an influencer, companies will offer you deals and opportunities to make money because they need your audience. Be intentional about the ones you say yes to because your audience is more valuable than any money a company offers. Always think long-term and ever think about what's best for your audience.

What kind of income can you make from influencer partnerships?

Depending on the size of your audience and the budget of the company or business you work with, you can earn a few hundred bucks to shoot one video or thousands of dollars to run a specific campaign over an agreed-upon timeframe.

Influencer marketing requires planning, strategy, and a solid business plan so you can get paid what you're worth.

SELL PRODUCTS AND MERCHANDISE OF YOUR BRAND

Another cool way to earn money as a YouTuber content creator is to create your merch. These can be T-shirts with your brand, coffee mugs, calendars, art, paintings, comics, recipes, or whatever else you can create for your niche. The best part about this is that you get to keep 100% of the profit. Use platforms like Shopify and Amazon to quickly set up shop then leverage your growing audience to drive traffic to your online store.

CROWDFUND YOU YOUTUBE PROJECT

If you're not looking to support your YouTube career with ads, affiliate marketing, and selling merch, you could go the crowdfunding route. Some have found it extremely success-ful. Unlike ads, you are giving your audience more of what they want. The focus here is content and engagement. Check out a channel like Hasfit, which mainly grew and still focuses on crowdfunding. You can crowdfund your channel through websites like Patreon or use the YouTube Sponsor Button, a newly established feature that lets your fans support your channel in exchange for some "perks" you give.

FAN FUNDING

As the word states, this is a way for your fans and subscribers to tip and support your hard work. The more great content you produce, the more likely you will build fans that love and appreciate all the effort and dedication you put in to serve them. If you want to create an easy way for people to "tip" you, then consider checking out a site like ko-fi.com, enabling you to receive tips or donations. You can also create a simple PayPal button that people can use to "buy you coffee" if they love your content and channel. Don't forget to make it easy for people to give you their cash by placing links on the description under each video.

SOCIAL MEDIA MARKETING ON YOUTUBE

Social media marketing uses social media platforms to connect with an audience to market your products. You can use social media marketing to grow your YouTube channel and sell products or services if you get the right strategy.

The strategy can be both paid and organic marketing efforts, but I suggest using some paid social media advertising if you want to see results fast.

One way you can make money on YouTube using social media marketing is by running ads on Instagram and Facebook that drives traffic back to your channel. You could also create a social media campaign offering a free lead magnet that leads to people sharing their data with you. Once you have that data, you can send people to your YouTube channel to promote whatever product or service you wish to sell, or they can be served ads through your YPP. If you'd like to learn more about social media marketing, which is a deep and vast topic, I suggest getting one of my other guides.

APPLYING YOUTUBE ON YOU EXISTING BUSINESS

The benefits of integrating YouTube into your business marketing and development strategies are too numerous to mention. Let's start with the fact that your Search Engine Optimization efforts will exponentially pay off when you leverage video marketing. As the second-largest search engine on the Internet, having your videos ranking high on Google will drive more traffic to your website. You will also develop an instant connection with your audience. Existing customers and prospects will feel more connected to your brand when you use videos to educate, inspire, and showcase your products. We know content marketing is here to stay because today's consumer prefers to learn about a product, feature, or brand through sharable, informative content instead of traditional dry ads. By choosing to create great videos, you're serving your potential customers' needs far better than your competitors, who might still be focused on traditional ads. I also believe that video marketing makes it easy for anyone with any budget to succeed because it's no longer about throwing money at ads to manipulate people into making a purchase. People want to feel valued, and with video, you can show your audience that you care and that your product or service is the best solution. I cannot think of a better way to market to an existing or new audience than through video content and a great YouTube channel.

YOUTUBE ADVERTISING

YouTube ads are great for attracting a customer or new subscribers to your channel if you have the budget. Introduce your brand or business using YouTube ads, and your channel will grow exponentially. But you can't just throw money into this. Make sure you have a solid plan with clear objectives before spending a dime. YouTube isn't as inexpensive as Facebook and Instagram because it's a mature platform, so the learning curve necessary to pull off a great campaign is steep. Luckily, they have many resources, educational content, and even a certification process to empower you to use their powerful advertising features. You can go from knowing absolutely nothing about Google ads to setting up a successful ad campaign in no time with as little as $10 per day.

There are several options when it comes to ads. You can create skippable in-stream ads, non-skippable in-stream ads (including bumper ads), video discovery ads, and non-video ads (the overlays and banners).

To advertise on YouTube, you will need to upload a video and set it on Public or Unlisted. Then sign in to your Google Ads account and select New Campaign. You will need to choose your goal (sales, website traffic, brand awareness, reach, or brand consideration. Please define your campaign parameters and budget, target your audience, and enter your link to hit the create campaign. And that's it! Your ad is live and ready to bring you a new audience.

To get the most out of your campaigns, use storytelling and emotion to connect with your audience. Have an appropriate call to action and consider using the right type of ad for the specific goal. For example, if sales were your main objective, I would recommend setting up a TrueView for an action campaign. That will allow you multiple clickable elements so viewers can click and take action before the video ends.

It's also a good idea to stick to the recommended length and video formats. Skippable ads should be minimum of 12 seconds and a maximum of 3 minutes (you can have a max of 60seconds on YouTube, kids). Non-skippable ads are 15seconds (In Singapore, Mexico, India, Malaysia, and EMEA, they allow 20seconds), and bumper ads are 6seconds.

For discovery ads, YouTube recommends having AVI, ASF, QuickTime, Windows Media, MP4, or MPEG file format. The video codec should be H.264, MPEG-2, or MPEG-4. The audio codec should be AAC-LC or MP3. The aspect ratio should be 16:9 or 4:3, and the frame rate most recommended is 30 FPS.

ACTIVITY #12: OPTIMIZATION

You've made it to the last activity for this book. Here, it's all about optimization. So far, you've learned how to take your growing channel and turn it into an income-generating machine. Take some time to decide on the avenues you will use to earn money and set up the necessary processes. If you're getting into influencer marketing, get a book and learn how to pitch, sell, and win deals with brands. You'll need to learn how to market yourself so that brands find you appealing.

If you're getting into affiliate marketing or creating and selling your own products, that will require some action steps that you need to plot and implement. Use this time to figure out how you can take action on those activities that will generate you money. You will also need to keep tweaking, iterating, and improving your channel's SEO. Keep monitoring and tracking everything as you publish new content so that your channel can turn into a profitable YouTube business.

CONCLUSION

You have made it to the end of this book. We've given you lots of material and assignments to work with so don't feel overwhelmed. Each section of this book was placed in the specific order that you will need to follow as a beginner.

The monetization section came last with good reason. A mistake many new YouTubers make is to focus on monetization too early in the game. As you put down this book, your main work is to implement the first three sections to the best of your ability. If you can get that done, monetization will be a natural by-product, and you will succeed.

You will not get very far if you don't develop the right mindset, discipline, persistence, and consistency necessary for this journey. Again, let me remind you that your WHY must be bigger than your obstacles, and the insecurities and doubts that will pop up along this journey. Your passion and desire to share your message, build a community, and serve others will determine how far you can go as a YouTuber.

The YouTube platform is one of the most powerful vehicles at your disposal in 2021, where you can be, do, give, and share whatever you believe in. Done right, it will open up opportunities and rewards beyond your wildest dreams. Many have started with an idea, built a brand over a long time, and turned a sad story into a YouTube empire. You have the potential to do the same. All you need is a plan. Each chapter of this book has given you that guideline and plan from setting up the channel to thinking through and researching content to finding your brand's identity and posting your first video.

You have learned hacks that will save you time and energy when it comes to editing and putting out professional-looking videos, even if you're shooting from a basement. What you need now is a serious commitment to your dream. If you are ready to be a successful YouTuber, it's time to put in the effort and reap the benefits of having thousands or millions of people watching your content, taking your advice, and buying things from you. Whatever your end goal might be - a lifestyle of travel, sharing your passion with the world, becoming famous, earning a six-figure income, boosting your local business, or any other objective, the first step is to implement the lessons this book offers.

To your YouTube success.

Brandon.

RESOURCES

Ubersuggest's Free Keyword Tool, Generate More Suggestions. (2020, April 17). Retrieved October 21, 2020, from https://neilpatel.com/ubersuggest/

YouTube, Twitch, Twitter, & Instagram Statistics - Social-Blade.com. (n.d.). Retrieved from https://socialblade.com/

Southern, M. (2020, June 29). Google Explains How YouTube Search Works. Retrieved October 21, 2020, from https://www.searchenginejournal.com/google-explains-how-youtube-search-works/373189/

Filmmaker, D. (2019, November 10). Should I Start a YouTube Channel? We Asked These YouTube Creators Their Advice. Retrieved October 21, 2020, from https://digitalfilmmaker.net/start-youtube-channel/

T. (2020e, May 25). 10 Most Popular and Profitable YouTube Niche Ideas. Retrieved October 21, 2020, from https://toughnickel.com/self-employment/10-Most-Profitable-YouTube-Niche-Ideas

Google Tool Find My Audience. (n.d.). Retrieved October 21, 2020, from https://www.thinkwithgoogle.com/feature/findmyaudience

Customize channel layout - YouTube Help. (n.d.). Retrieved October 21, 2020, from https://support.google.com/youtube/answer/3219384?hl=en&visit_id=637391251673478626-2441383931&rd=1

Segev, L. (2020, August 26). The Importance of Branding for YouTube Creators: TubeTalk Episode 161. Retrieved October 21, 2020, from https://vidiq.com/blog/post/branding-for-youtube-creators-tubetalk-161/

Proud, D. (2020, February 13). Proud Business Productions - How To Customise Your YouTube Channel Layout. Retrieved October 21, 2020, from https://www.proudbusinessproductions.com/blog/2020/2/21/how-to-customise-your-youtube-channel-layout

Gardner, K. (2020, September 3). Quality is in the eye of the beholder: new research on what viewers love. Retrieved October 21, 2020, from https://www.thinkwithgoogle.com/marketing-strategies/video/video-production-quality/

Google. (2016, September). *Deep Neural Networks For YouTube Recommendations.* Paul Covington, Jay Adams, Emre Sargin. Retrieved from https://static. googleusercontent.com/media/research.google.com/en// pubs/archive/45530.pdf

Discover video traffic sources - YouTube Help. (n.d.). Retrieved October 21, 2020, from https://support.google. com/youtube/answer/9314355?hl=en

Vidcon Event. (n.d.). Retrieved October 21, 2020, from https://www.vidcon.com/

CPSIA information can be obtained
at www.ICGtesting.com
Printed in the USA
BVHW011633250721
612718BV00022B/553